DYLAN THOMAS
Letters to Vernon Watkins

Vernon. With love from Dylan. 1935.

DYLAN THOMAS
Letters to Vernon Watkins

edited

with an introduction

by

VERNON WATKINS

J. M. DENT AND SONS LIMITED
Aldine House, Bedford Street, London, W.C.2
and
FABER AND FABER LIMITED
24 Russell Square, London, W.C.1

First published in mcmlvii
by J. M. Dent and Sons Limited
Aldine House, Bedford Street, London, W.C.2
and Faber and Faber Limited
24 Russell Square, London, W.C.1
Printed in Great Britain by
Western Printing Services Ltd, Bristol

CONTENTS

ACKNOWLEDGEMENTS

In some cases, where the context seemed to warrant it, I asked people mentioned in these letters for permission to print their names. I am grateful to those who gave their consent. My thanks are also due to Mrs. Dylan Thomas for permission to print her letter, and to Robert Fitzgerald and New Directions for the reproduction of the poem 'Evening Prayer' by Robert Fitzgerald, quoted by Dylan Thomas in an early letter.

V. W.

INTRODUCTION

When I think of Dylan Thomas's letters to me I include also those letters which I have lost, and my impression is of an unbroken commentary on his poems from the time when he was putting his second book *Twenty-Five Poems* together until the publication of *Deaths and Entrances*. Two or three poems in *Deaths and Entrances* were not sent to me, and 'Fern Hill' was one of these; but almost all the others were accompanied by letters. It will be seen from the chronological arrangement of the letters that there are none between the end of 1941 and 1944. I left for the Air Force in December 1941. Just before leaving I gathered together what letters I could see, lying about everywhere in an accumulation which had no method, and filed them away. It is to that gesture of orderliness that I owe the survival of so many early letters. Even so, some which were of extraordinary interest and some which were very funny disappeared. There was one describing his own medical examination for the Army and another describing his reactions to mine which were unforgettably comic. Even a general could not have taken them in his pocket with safety—the strain would have been too great.

Between 1942 and 1944 I stayed with Dylan frequently in London on short leave-passes from my station. The years, in fact, which are not here represented by letters, were years when we saw each other more often than at any time since he left Swansea. The letters that came then were often mere notes arranging to meet, the discussion of poems being postponed until the meeting, when the exact analysis of his written self-criticism gave way to the concise and lightning judgments of his conversation. It was from his own lips that I heard for the first time his poem 'A Refusal to Mourn' before it was finally formed.

Memory plays tricks with imagination and imagination with memory. When, at the beginning of 1946, I left the Air Force and returned to Swansea, I remembered the file of letters which had remained untouched for so long. That part of the correspondence which discussed poetry I remembered clearly, and on this subject I expected to find more letters than I found; but the letters on other subjects had been transmuted by memory into conversation, and I was delighted to find that so many conversations had been written down. These, in turn, reminded me of others which I did not find, for handwriting is a great restorer of memory. The balance was, however, lucky and good, considering that the preservation of the letters was so accidental. The richness of the letters I was now re-reading brought back to me, with the atmosphere of pre-war Swansea and Laugharne, a situation, an era and an excitement which cannot be repeated. Not even the stories in the *Portrait of the Artist as a Young Dog* can serve the memory so well as these.

We met a few months after his first book, *Eighteen Poems*, had been published. I remember turning over the pages of the book in the bookshop where it was prominently displayed, with a curiosity which was mingled with a determination not to buy it. Then I ran into his uncle whom I had known when I was a child, and he gave me his address. Soon after this I called at the house at the top of Cwmdonkin Drive, high above Swansea, and his mother told me that he was expected back from London in a few days. We arranged that as soon as he arrived he should come out to see me. In a few weeks, on the day after his return, he arrived.

He was slight, shorter than I had expected, shy, rather flushed and eager in manner, deep-voiced, restless, humorous, with large, wondering, yet acutely intelligent eyes, gold curls, snub nose, and the face of a cherub. I quickly realized when we went for a walk on the cliffs that this cherub took nothing for granted. In thought and words he was anarchic, challenging, with the certainty of that instinct which knows its own freshly discovered truth.

We became close friends almost immediately, from an affinity which I think we both recognized at once. That affinity was particularly clear when we talked about poetry or read it aloud; yet our approach to it and our way of working presented a complete contrast. Dylan worked upon a symmetrical abstract with tactile delicacy; out of a lump of texture or nest of phrases he created music, testing everything by physical feeling, working from the concrete image outwards. I worked from music and cadence towards the density of physical shape. I worked at night, he in the day, usually in the afternoon, but never in the evening which he regarded as the social time of the day. I used titles; he did not; but I did eventually persuade him to use them. At first he saw no reason why a poet should use a title any more than a composer, and he disliked what seemed to him an unnecessary label of simplification. Later, the title itself was able to give him a measure of excitement without which the measure of the poem would be incomplete.

My first impression of a rooted obstinacy, which was really a rooted innocence, was reinforced whenever we met. We met often, either at his house or mine. At our first meeting at my house I had read poems of my own; on the first evening I spent with him at Cwmdonkin Drive he began to read his. He unfolded a large file, marked in block letters POMES. The first poem he read to me was 'Ears in the Turrets Hear', and he followed this with others which he intended to print in his second book, *Twenty-five Poems*. Last of all he read the sonnet sequence, of which he had then written seven, beginning 'Altar-wise by Owl-light in the Half-way House'. He looked up on reading the last line:

On rose and icicle the ringing handprint.

It was not many weeks before he added three more sonnets, on the Crucifixion, Egyptian burial, and the Resurrection, to the sequence. He intended to write more and make it a much

13

longer work, but the sequence of ten sonnets was all he completed, and that is how it appears in his *Collected Poems*.

Besides poetry, Dylan read me stories. One of the first he read was 'The Orchards', printed in the *Faber Book of Modern Stories* and afterwards collected with other early stories in his third book, *The Map of Love*. It was in this story that the trick-name Llareggub first appeared. Dylan alone could have devised so Welsh an invention, but it was also an example of the word-play he had learnt from Joyce, his most admired prose writer, whose 'Dubliners' made him deprecate his own short stories. 'Llareggub' became, much later, the provisional title of 'Under Milk Wood', and was printed as such in the first version, half of which was published in *Botteghe Oscure* in 1952.

Dylan showed me the manuscript of 'The Orchards'. The whole story was written in minute handwriting on the inside cover of a cardboard box. He told me that it helped him to see the whole story in one place as he wrote it, and pages were less good for this than box-covers. Some of the stories showed an almost surrealist imagination, but this did not appear in the poems, and as an influence on his work it did not last long. He did, though, enjoy the Surrealist Exhibition in 1935, where a learned lecture was given in a packed room accompanied by an electric bell which made every word inaudible. Everyone had been asked to do something, he said. He had himself boiled string and offered it to people in cups with polite 'weak or strong?' words.

Another story Dylan read me at this time was 'The Lemon', which *Life and Letters* afterwards printed. In this he explored almost scientifically the link or skin between the interior and exterior worlds, for the two were still mysteriously separated in his imagination, and in both his poetry and his prose he was still much more conscious of the first than of the second. But the best story of this period was one which he read me while it was still in the course of composition. It was to be called 'A View of the Sea', and was to be dedicated to his friend Tom Warner who had written a piece of music with that title. Tom

14

Warner was one of several friends who used to meet Dylan regularly at the Kardomah in Swansea every Wednesday during my lunch-hour; Alfred Janes, the painter, another very close friend, was invariably there, and one or two story-writers and journalists came almost as often. Dylan was always ready to accept suggestions when he read aloud. He would return to them afterwards, testing them many times on his tongue. In this particular story one or two small alterations were made, and one of these made it necessary to change the title, which became 'A Prospect of the Sea'.

Dylan was now preparing his second book of poems, *Twenty-five Poems*, and they were almost finished. He liked these poems, for the most part, much better than the poems of his first book. He read me the first long poem, 'I, in my Intricate Image', a poem in three parts which has seventy-two variations in line-endings on the letter '1', twenty-four in each part. While he read the poem I did not notice this, which is so obvious to the eye, so subtle was the use of the variations and so powerful the poem's progress. He said afterwards that he did not think it a successful poem, but that he liked it as well as anything he had written up to that time. The statement was modest, but Dylan was always modest about his poems, though he was really very sure of them. It was characteristic of his taste at that time that his favourite lines in the poem were these:

I with the wooden insect in the tree of nettles,
In the glass bed of grapes with snail and flower,
Hearing the weather fall.

Other poems of the book which he was just finishing were 'Then Was My Neophyte' and 'To-day this Insect and the World I Breathe', both of which came out in the Autumn 1936 number of the magazine *Purpose*. Edith Sitwell had in the *London Mercury* written about the beautiful poem 'A Grief Ago', and her praise was the first really emphatic eulogy of Dylan's poetry to reach the public. Besides confessing the excitement and overwhelming effect the poem had produced when she read it, she gave an analysis of its parts, investigating its mysterious force through sound-values, and attempting to sift its compound images. With her siftings of meaning Dylan did not altogether agree, but he did appreciate her genuine response to the poem. He always spoke of her with affection, and when, later, there was a series of letters in a Sunday paper attacking his poetic method it was she who brilliantly answered them. Dylan himself never wrote; but after one particularly insulting letter from a member of the Athenaeum Club, he asked me whether the paper would print a letter asking the member to meet him on the steps of the Athenaeum so that he could hit him.

I tried to persuade Dylan to leave two of the poems out of the new book of *Twenty-five*. These were the poems beginning 'Now, Say Nay . . .' and 'How Soon the Servant Sun'. The other poems all seemed packed with meaning, but for me these two poems presented a face of unwarrantable obscurity. He himself remarked of one of them that so far as he knew it had no meaning at all. He was, however, firm about including them. When I said that reviewers would be likely to pick these out rather than the fine poems in the book he smiled and said, 'Give them a bone.'

The one poem which Dylan hesitated to include in *Twenty-five Poems* was one which afterwards became very well known. When I called at Cwmdonkin Drive one evening he said that he had almost decided to leave out 'And Death Shall Have No Dominion'. Certainly he would leave it out unless he altered it. He read it aloud many times, and I said how necessary it was to the book and how much I admired it, especially its impulsive rhythm. He made a number of small changes that evening, and when I left my head was full of the excitement of the finished poem.

The only other revisions I remember Dylan making were in the 'neophyte' poem where a single word was altered, and in the poem 'Should Lanterns Shine', where I persuaded him to

16

cut the last two lines of the poem as it had appeared in *New Verse*. These two lines,

> *Regard the moon, it hangs above the lawn;*
> *Regard the lawn, it lies beneath the moon.*

seemed to me to echo Eliot, and indirectly Laforgue, and not to belong to the poem, whereas the two previous lines, with their hidden nuances, made a fine autobiographical ending:

> *The ball I threw while playing in the park*
> *Has not yet reached the ground.*

From this time forward Dylan sent me his poems more or less as he finished them. I typed them for him, and we discussed them in letters if we could not see each other. I typed all the poems for his next book, *The Map of Love*, containing poems and stories, which was published by Dent in 1939. The excitement I felt when I opened these poems was always great, and they usually came one at a time. He was a slow and patient craftsman, and he had become slower since the early poems. His method of composition was itself painfully slow. He used separate work-sheets for individual lines, sometimes a page or two being devoted to a single line, while the poem was gradually built up, phrase by phrase. He usually had beforehand an exact conception of the poem's length, and he would decide how many lines to allot to each part of its development. In spite of the care and power and symmetry of its construction, he recognized at all times that it was for the sake of divine accidents that a poem existed at all.

Dylan shared my admiration of Yeats whom he considered the greatest living poet; but Hardy was his favourite poet of the century. He disliked the sociological poetry of the thirties. My own themes were really closer to his; we were both religious poets, and neither of us had any aptitude for political reform. He understood, too, why I could never write a poem dominated by time, as Hardy could. This, in fact, was also true of Dylan, though some critics have mistakenly thought to find such poems in his work. It illustrates our affinity on a deeper level: his poems spoke to me with the voice of metaphysical truth; if we disagreed it was on a metaphysical issue, for natural observation in poetry meant nothing to us without the support of metaphysical truth.

Dylan admired W. H. Auden's versatility, both his depth and his wit, but at that time he usually disliked his themes. I remember particularly one morning when we met in the Kardomah with Alfred Janes and John Prichard, the story-writer and poet. He said that the Editor of *New Verse* had asked him for a tribute to Auden for an Auden double-number of the magazine which he was preparing. What should he say? He sent a short tribute, full of enthusiastic praise, but added a Postscript: 'Congratulations on Auden's seventieth birthday.'

From this point forward the letters can, I think, best illustrate themselves. I find that the first I have preserved was sent in April 1936. I seem to have lost all the letters that came between that date and the following summer. In the early summer Keidrych Rhys, whom I had already met in Swansea, launched his magazine *Wales*, which was to print a good deal of the Anglo-Welsh writing in poetry and prose later collected in books and anthologies. For the first number Dylan had himself collected several contributions including two of my poems, 'Old Triton Time' and 'Griefs of the Sea'. My efforts to persuade him to use titles were countered by his efforts to persuade me to send a poem to a magazine. In the end both were successful, but not without some recrimination. He had picked up my poems on a visit to my house and I now looked forward to seeing them; but when *Wales* appeared 'Griefs of the Sea' had been altered, one line being left out and, I think, two others changed. We had always agreed to suggest any improvement to each other in a poem where it seemed to go wrong, and in this particular poem Dylan had persuaded me to make one change of a word, but to alter a poem without the other's consent was to me unthinkable. I wrote a letter which began with a curse, and in a few days I had the gentlest of replies with the news that he had just been married; so my blessing instantly followed. The task of altering the pile of copies of *Wales* in the bookshop was laborious and illicit, but I did it in the next few days. When my first book appeared four years later the original version was restored: the valuable word Dylan had given me in conversation was there; the alterations he had made away from me were not.

The regrettable fact that no letters from me have been preserved makes certain passages in the correspondence difficult to understand; but I have tried to remedy these patches of obscurity with notes. I am saved a good deal of embarrassment by the knowledge that some of my more stupid suggestions for improving a line are in limbo, but I would gladly endure it for the sake of clarifying every facet of Dylan's replies. As it is, there is a rightness in all his intuitive statements about poetry and an honesty in his destructive criticism which make these letters the closest commentary on his own poems that will ever be written.

The advent of war filled Dylan with horror, and the war itself was a nightmare from which he never completely recovered. But for a tribunal at which he had to be a witness he would certainly have asked to be registered as a conscientious objector; but the attitude of the conscientious objectors themselves had also impressed him: he would never, he said, object on religious grounds. So he registered for the Army 'as a never-fighter', as he put it in one of the letters which is not here.

Just before the war I stayed with Dylan frequently in Laugharne. The peace and beauty of this small sea-town beyond Carmarthen, a fishing village at the end of the world, represented for him the last refuge of life and sanity in a nightmare world, the last irregular protest against the regularity and symmetry of madness.

My visits to Laugharne, like my earlier visits to Dylan's parents' house in Swansea, and to that smaller house in

Bishopston to which they moved after his father's retirement, where Dylan and Caitlin would stay, were always extremely happy, overshadowed though they were by the expectation of war. The calmest and happiest days of his life were probably those he spent in Wales. The chief part of his creative writing was done in the landscape and among the people to whom he was most deeply attached. He was able in Laugharne to work continuously almost every afternoon. In London, where he had so many social contacts and where so many dramatic masks were expected of him, he could not work at all.

The letters, which to me present a background of so much life, and which seem to me the richest letters of our time, are so vivid that I am printing them as fully as possible. If every word in them were printed no harm would be done, for there can never have been a correspondence so intense as this and yet so completely free from malice. Only in two or three instances have I left out a passage or personal reference which might be misconstrued. Names are sometimes omitted, from a tact which is perhaps unwarranted. Dylan delighted always to express himself in extravagant statement, and the extravagance, which was often directed against himself, was a true reflection of instinct. Sense and nonsense, it was all organic, and belonged to himself.

The point of balance in the letters is perhaps 1939, the year in which he abandoned the struggling, symbol-charged prose of the intensely subjective early stories and began to write stories about human beings living and behaving exactly as they used to live and behave when he was a child. These were the stories of his *Portrait of the Artist as a Young Dog*. Once he had begun to write about real people he found that he did not want to return to the other style. I remember him saying at this time of an early story: 'I shall never write a story of that kind again.' Just as Yeats had announced his change to a bare style in his little poem 'The Coat', so Dylan had already anticipated this change in his short poem about Cwmdonkin Park which begins:

> *Once it was the colour of saying*
> *Soaked my table the uglier side of a hill.*

I give it here, sent with the letter of 29 December, 1938. Both in poetry and prose his work from this time forward moved in the direction of the living voice.

It was inevitable that there should be fewer letters after the war. Except for picking out odd ones for particular friends I did not read the letters consecutively until six months ago; certainly I did not have them in any kind of order until then. Some found their way into the wrong envelopes and others had no envelope or date at all. Two recent letters have been lost, one a long one of great interest; the other a short one, almost entirely personal, disappeared last year. It was after finding that I had lost this that I decided, last November, to copy those that remained. Only when I had finished copying did I feel that a decision I had earlier made not to publish the letters was mistaken.

VERNON WATKINS

June 1956

Polgigga, Porthcurno, Penzance, Cornwall
Monday [Envelope dated 20th April, 1936]
Dear Vernon,

Perhaps it's a bit late to say Sorry for not having let you know I couldn't come to see you that particular Sunday—whenever it was—and to tell you how much I missed you and the unwonted walk and the toasted things for tea and the poetry after it; but I want to say Sorry, and I hope you'll forgive me, and I hope, though that's the wrong way of putting it, that you missed your hearty, Britain-chested, cliff-striding companion as much as I did. I had crowds of silly, important things to do: pack, write formal letters, gather papers, and catch the Sunday night train; and I didn't get out of bed until all those things had to be scamped through. Now in a hundred ways I wish I hadn't come away; I'm full of nostalgia and a frightful cold; here the out-of-doors is very beautiful, but it's a strange country to me, all scenery and landscape, and I'd rather the bound slope of a suburban hill, the Elms, the Acacias, Rookery Nook, Curlew Avenue, to all these miles of green fields and flowery cliffs and dull sea going on and on, and cows lying down and down. I'm not a country man; I stand for, if anything, the aspidistra, the provincial drive, the morning cafe, the evening pub; I'd like to believe in the wide open spaces as the wrapping around walls, the windy boredom between house and house, hotel and cinema, bookshop and tube-station; man made his house to keep the world and the weather out, making his own weathery world inside; that's the trouble with the country: there's too much public world between private ones. And living in your own private, four-walled world as exclusively as possible isn't escapism, I'm sure; it isn't the Ivory Tower, and, even if it were, you secluded in your Tower

23

know and learn more of the world outside than the outside-man who is mixed up so personally and inextricably with the mud and the unlovely people—(sorry, old Christian)—and the four bloody muddy winds. |

I was in London for just over a week, and the same things happened there that always happen: I kept roughly a half of my appointments, met half the people I wanted to, met lots of other people, desirable and otherwise, and fully lived up to the conventions of Life No. 13: promiscuity, booze, coloured shirts, too much talk, too little work. I had Nights Out with those I always have Nights Out with: Porteous, Cameron, Blakeston, Grigson, and old Bill Empson and all—(Empson, by the way, has been very kind to me in print, in a review of the Faber anthology, saying, quite incorrectly, though than which etc. there could be nothing nicer for my momentary vanity, that little or nothing of importance, except for Owen and Eliot, comes between Eliot and ME. Ho! Ha!) Also I had lunch with Pope Eliot, as I said I would have; he *was* charming, a great man, I think, utterly unaffected; I had a spot of rheumatism that day, and nearly the whole time was spent in discussing various methods of curing it, ("I think it was in 1927 I had my worst bout, and I tried Easu Ointment" etc). I left London with Life No. Thirteen's headache, liver, and general seediness, and have by this time thoroughly recovered.

Polgigga is a tiny place two miles or less from Land's End, and very near Penzance and Mousehole (really the loveliest village in England). We live here in a cottage in a field, with a garden full of ferrets and bees. Every time you go to the garden lavatory you are in danger of being stung or bitten. My hostess, or what you like, has unfortunately read too many books of psychology, and talks about my ego over breakfast; her conversation is littered with phrases like narcissist fixation and homosexual transference; she is a very simple person who tries to cure her simplicity by a science which, in its turn, tries to cure the disease it suffers from. I don't think that's my phrase, but here in this Freudian house it's truer than hell.

24

One day, though never in a letter, I must tell you the whole silly, strange story behind all this—this most irregular, unequal Cornwall partnership; I don't think for a moment that you'll enjoy it, and I know that you'll agree with me how wrong, if there can be any values here, I was to begin it. But I *shall* tell you probably when I see you in the summer—a summer I'm looking forward to a lot. The one thing that's saving me—saving me, I mean, not from any melodramatic issues but just from sheer unhappiness—is lots and lots of work. I'm half way through another story, and have more or less finished a poem which I want to send you when I'm better pleased with it. But here again I'm not free; perhaps, as you said once, I should stop writing altogether for some time; now I'm almost afraid of all the once-necessary artifices and obscurities, and can't, for the life or the death of me, get any real liberation, any diffusion or dilution or anything, into the churning bulk of the words; I seem, more than ever, to be tightly packing away everything I have and know into a mad-doctor's bag, and then locking it up: all you can see is the bag, all you can know is that it's full to the clasp, all you have to trust is that the invisible and intangible things packed away are—if they *could* only be seen and touched—worth quite a lot. I don't really know why I should be unloading any of this on you, and probably boring you—no, that's wrong, you couldn't be one of the bored ones of the world—at the same time. But you are—even if only momentarily—the one happy person I know, the one who, contrary to facts and, in a certain way, to circumstances, seems to be almost entirely uncomplicated: not, either, the uncomplication of a beginning person, but that of a person who has worked through all the beginnings and finds himself a new beginning in the middle—I hope, for your today's happiness, —a beginning at the end. That's not clear, of course. You might, and would, I know, if you could, help me by talking to me. I don't fear—we talked about it, do you remember—any sudden cessation or drying-up, any coming to the end, any (sentimentally speaking) putting out of the fires; what I do fear is an ingrowing, the impulse growing like a toenail into the artifice. Talk to me about it, will you—it's probably a terrible task I'm trying to drag you into—in any way, any words. And tell me what you're doing and writing. I'll write you again soon, a clearer letter, less face-in-the-earth, less eye-in-a-sling.

Yours always,
DYLAN.

God, I almost forgot.

Are you rich temporarily? Would you like to lend me some money, a pound or, at the very most, two pounds? I have a beastly, vital debt—rather a lot—to pay in the next few days; I've got together most of it, but not quite all, and all has to be paid. I can—if you *are* penniful temporarily, and, if you're not, do forget it and go on writing the long letter you're going to write to me—let you have it back next week certainly. Of course you don't mind me asking you, but if you're broke or holiday-saving, I can get a few pounds elsewhere—though not, Mr. Watkins, with such lack of embarrassment as I can ask you for it.

Yours always again,
D.

[*Pencil P.S.*]
Did the snaps—I bet they didn't—come out well, or at all?

My letter, to which the following letter is an answer, had begun:
' This is just to wish you an extra sweat in your worst nightmare
for altering ' Griefs of the Sea'.' It was Dylan Thomas's slightly
altered version, one line being inverted and another left out, which
appeared in the first number of Keidrych Rhys's magazine Wales.

Lobster Pot, Mousehole, Cornwall, 15th July 1937
I'm sorry that this is such a
short and inadequate letter. I'll
do much better next time.

Dear Vernon,

If, in some weeks' time, you see a dog-like shape with a torn
tail and a spaniel eye, its tail between its legs, come cringing
and snuffling up Heatherslade gravel, it will be me; look carefully at its smarmy rump that asks to be kicked, its trembling,
penholding paw that scribbles, "kick me", in the dust. It will
deserve your anger. But, really, the Grief of the Sea was this:
I was fooling about with a copy of the poem, playing the
pleasant, time-wasting game of altering, unasked-for, somebody else's work; and then, when I met Keidrych with the
manuscripts I had collected, blindly and carelessly I must have
included among them the for-my-own-benefit, not-to-be-
shown copy instead of the original. I hope you forgive me:
that's the truth. I was worried when I saw the first number of
Wales, with that Thowdlerized version in it, and should, anyway, in a few days have sent off an explanation to you. Further
than that I Cannot Go, but you may still kick me when we
meet in Pennard again—and I'm hoping that will be soon.

Yes I thought "Wales" was good, too. I had actually very
little myself to do with the editing, though when Keidrych goes
up to Cambridge next year I shall probably—and with you as
colleague, or whatever it is, if you'd be—take it all over. And
no more —— when we do: he can crawl back into the wood-
work, or lift up his stone again.

My own news is very big and simple. I was married three
days ago; to Caitlin Macnamara; in Penzance registry office;
with no money, no prospect of money, no attendant friends or
relatives, and in complete happiness. We've been meaning to
from the first day we met, and now we are free and glad. We're
moving next week—for how long depends on several things,
but mostly on one—to a studio some miles away, in Newlyn,
a studio above a fish-market & where gulls fly in to breakfast.

But I shall be trying to come home soon for at least a few days, along with Caitlin: I think you'll like [her] very much, she looks like the princess on the top of a Christmas tree, or like a stage Wendy; but, for God's sake, don't tell her that.

Write as soon as you can, and bless me.

Love to all the family.

Yours always,

DYLAN.

Dylan had now moved from Cornwall, and the next letters all come from Mrs. Macnamara's house at Ringwood where he was staying.

My poem 'Mana', printed afterwards in Ballad of the Mari Lwyd and Other Poems, *had originally a different opening line in which I had used 'fabled' as a verb. The line was, I remember:*

When the white smoke has fabled through the bones.

The reference to Francis at the end of this letter is to Francis Dufau-Labeyrie, a French friend whose translation of Portrait of the Artist as a Young Dog *was later published in the* Editions de Minuit. *After 1938 he did not see Dylan again until about three months before Dylan's death when he once more went with me to Laugharne.*

Blashford, Ringwood, Hants. [*No date: envelope dated 25th October 1937*]

Dear Vernon,

Thank you for the poems. I like them all. My respect for them is always increased when I read them again, and in typescript. "Mana" is magnificent, especially the fourth verse. At the moment, I think it's your best short poem. I still don't like the first line. Perhaps I never mentioned it, but from the beginning, from the first time I saw the poem shaping, I've felt the line to be wrong, disliked "fabled"—not because it is used as a verb, but because of its position—and felt uneasy about the rhythm. The rhythm is one that I myself have used to death, and my feeling against it is perhaps over-personal. The line is so stridently an opening line: tum tum tum, all the wheels and drums are put in motion: a poem is about to begin. I see the workman's clothes, I hear the whistle blowing in the poem-factory. And one other line I think is bad: "Laid in the long grey shadow of our weeping thought". This, to me, has far too many weak words. They are weak alone, & weaker when added together. They do not cancel each other out, though, but elongate a thin nothing: a long, grey, weeping sausage. But that's fancy talk. What I mean is, the whole line seems a kind of tired indrawing of breath between loud & strong utterances. And I've always disliked the weak line. I admit that readers of complicated poetry do need a breather every now and then, but I don't think the poetry should give it to them. When they want one, they should take it and then go on.

I don't know yet what I'll read at the Cardiff lecture, but I'll let you know beforehand: the Ballad certainly, After Sunset probably, one or two of the lyrics in 'Wales', and, perhaps, either Mana or Griefs of the Sea. And an Auden, a Ransome [sic], maybe Prokosch.

This is a very lovely place. Caitlin & I ride into the New Forest every day, into Bluebell Wood or onto Cuckoo Hill. There's no-one else about; Caitlin's mother is away; we are quiet and small and cigarette-stained and very young. I've read two dozen thrillers, the whole of Jane Austen, a new Wodehouse, some old Powys, a book of Turgenev, 3 lines by Gertrude Stein, & an anthology of Pure Poetry by George Moore. There are only about 2,000 books left in the house.

My poem is continuing. You shall have it next week. Regards to your mother and father. Remember me to Francis—to whom I *must* write. And have a nice week-end.

DYLAN.

[Here follow four deleted lines of verse]

This was a quotation from the new verse of my poem, which I've thought better about.

The poem discussed in the second paragraph of the next letter is his 'Poem to Caitlin', the second poem in The Map of Love, *reprinted in* Collected Poems. *I saw this poem at many stages on its way to completion. It took roughly a year to finish. A single line would occupy him for many days.*

Blashford, Ringwood, Hants., 13th November, 37

Dear Vernon,

Thank you for the new version of "Mana". I think it's very right now, don't you. I never really care to suggest actual, detailed alterations in anyone else's poem, (in spite of the apparently contradictory evidence of 'Griefs of the Sea'), but I'm glad you did alter the first line—(here-it-comes-boys)—and that line in the middle—(now-boys-take-a-deep-breath).

Here, after so long, is my own new poem. I hope you'll like it. I've used 'molten', as you suggested, but kept 'priest's grave foot', which is not, I'm sure, really ugly. In the last line of the seventh verse, you'll notice—'a man is tangled'. It was weeks after writing that line that I remembered Prokosch's 'man-entangled sea':* but I don't think any apologies are necessary, anyway. Lines 4 & 5 of the last verse might, perhaps, sound too fluent: I mean, they might sound as though they came too easily in a manner I have done my best to discard, but they say exactly what I mean them to. Are they clear? Once upon a time, before my death & resurrection, before the 'terrible' world had shown itself to me (however lyingly, as lines 6 & 7 of the last verse might indicate) as not so terrible

* From the poem 'The Baltic Shore' in *The Assassins* by Frederic Prokosch (Chatto and Windus, 1936).

after all, a wind had blown that had frightened everything &
created the first ice & the first frost by frightening the falling
snow so much that the blood of each flake froze. This is
probably clear, but, even to me, the lines skip (almost)
along so that they are taken too quickly, & then mainly by the
eye.

I wonder if you would type a couple of copies of the poem
for me—there's no typewriter within miles—and let me have
them as quickly as you can. I must get the poem off, and soon,
because I need, terribly urgently, the little money it will get
me.

News, though not much, when I write again. And I'll write
when I send off the poem to Eliot—(I want the Criterion to do
it). Don't forget, will you? And much love to you.

DYLAN.

P.S. It's a full stop after 'ice' in the last verse.
P.P.S. If I come to Cardiff to lecture—which is financially
improbable—I'll try to spend the night at Swansea. And see
you, of course.
P.P.S. Since writing this, I've done another little poem:
nothing at all important, or even (probably,) much good: just
a curious thought said quickly. I think it will be good for me
to write some short poems, not bothering about them too
much, between my long exhausters.

[*Enclosure:*]
The spire cranes. Its statue is an aviary.
From the stone nest it does not let the feathery
Carved birds blunt their striking throats on the salt gravel,
Pierce the spilt sky with diving wing in weed and heel
An inch in froth. Chimes cheat the prison statue, pelter
In time like outlaw rains on that priest, water,
Time for the swimmers' hands, music for silver lock
And mouth. Both note and plume plunge from the spire's hook.

Those craning birds are choice for you, songs that jump back
To the built voice, or fly with winter to the bells,
But do not travel down dumb wind like prodigals.

*The 'sixty-line-year's work' at the beginning of the next letter
refers to the 'Poem to Caitlin'. I had called the ending 'hurried'
in that version which he again worked on and altered considerably
before it was printed. The third sentence in the letter refers to a
poem I later abandoned.*

[*Undated: envelope dated 20th November, 1937. No address.*
from Blashford, Ringwood, Hants.]

Dear Vernon,

Thank you so much for the typewritten poems. I agree with
you entirely as to the (apparently) hurried ending of my sixty-
line-year's work, and will alter the middle lines of the last
verse. This should take me until Christmas, and my present to
you will be, inedibly, the revised and final copy. About go-
cripple-come-Michaelmas I'll write next time. At the moment,
though, I have another favour to ask. In ten days' time I am
to give a reading in the London University, reading alone with
no commentary. I scrapped the Cardiff lecture, as I had pre-
pared no grave speech and did not feel like travelling 200 miles
just to recite, in my fruity voice, poems that would not be
appreciated & could, anyway, be read in books. The London
affair, however, is at the request of a vague friend, & will have
to be fulfilled. I shall read you, me, Auden, Ransome [sic],
Prokosch, Yeats. I have plenty of me at hand, several of you,
& enough Auden. Will you assist me, tremendously too, by
telling me what of Yeats to read and—this is the favour, the
tiresome favour—copy out for me the poems you choose.

This house is stacked with books, but all prose, and I have
brought nothing with me but a few Penguin Shakespeares and
a pocket dictionary. I know it's a bother for you, but if you

could type for me—say, half a dozen Yeats (middle & late, including, if you think it as good as others, the one ending 'A terrible beauty is born', & the ones I know so little & that one you have read me)—it would be kind and splendid. It's too much to ask you also to copy out one Prokosch, but, if you have some spare minutes, could you do it? I want the reading to be of poems not *too* well known—with Yeats's exception, & Prokosch, I believe, is still only known as a dilletante [sic] name—outside the Criterion & one or two other papers of an established snob-appeal. The programme, roughly, I have in mind is: 'Dead Boy' & either 'Captain Carpenter' or 'Judith' —of Ransome; 'Prologue' & 'Ballad' of Auden; one good Prokosch; at least three Yeats; that tiny poem by Antonia White; John Short's Carol; Gavin Ewart's 'sexual insignia' poem; your Ballad of the Rough Sea, Griefs of the Sea, & Mana; my new poem, & two of the poems at the end of my last book. I shall read for, probably, 3/4 of an hour, explaining, of course, that my reading is not supposed to prove anything, and that my selection is based on nothing but a personal liking. The details of the programme I may alter. Anyway, do try to copy out those things as quickly as possible. I began this letter two days ago, & then, owing to the arrival of all sorts of odd people here, put off sending it until to-day. Now the time I have before the reading is alarmingly short; I've just realized the date to be the 27th. This is rudely rushing you, but could you type the Yeats—&, I hope very much, a Prokosch by about Wednesday. It's blackmail to say I'm relying on you, but I crookedly am. I respect your judgement, & your typing. Love & admiration as always,

DYLAN.

The next letter suggested my poem 'Portrait of a Friend', based on Dylan's own photograph which forms the frontispiece of this book, and which was sent to me, imperfectly packed, with the

PORTRAIT OF A FRIEND

He has sent me this
Late and early page
Caught in the emphasis
Of last night's cartonnage,
Crumpled in the post,
Bringing to lamplight
Breath's abatement,
Over- and under-statement,
Mute as a mummy's pamphlet
Long cherished by a ghost.

Who for annunciation has
The white wings of the sheldrake,
Labouring water's praise,
The blind shriek of the mandrake,
Broken shells for story,
Torn earth for love's near head
Raised from time's estuary,
Fed by the raven's bread;
A trespasser in tombs,
He bids the grey dust fall,
Groans in the shaping limbs:
'All stars are in my shawl.'
Who feels the deathbound sighs,
Mocks the Winged Horse's fake,
Toiling, as with closed eyes,
Love's language to remake,
To draw from their dumb wall
The saints to a wordly brothel
That a sinner's tongue may toll
And call the place Bethel.

34

Trusting a creaking house,
His roof is ruinous,
So mortal. A real wind
Beats on this house of sand
Two tides like ages buffet.
The superhuman, crowned
Saints must enter this drowned
Tide-race of the mind
To guess or understand
The face of this cracked prophet,
Which from its patient pall
I slowly take,
Drop the envelope,
Compel his disturbing shape,
And write these words on a wall
Maybe for a third man's sake.

Blashford, Ringwood, Hants., 7th February [*1938*]
Dear Vernon,
   I haven't written to you for such a long time. I don't know,
even, if I thanked you for the typewriting of those Yeats,
Prokosch, & Watkins poems. If I didn't, I'm ashamed. And,
ashamed or not, thank you very much. And for the jack-in-
the-box at Christmas: it frightened us all: we opened it late
at night, when we were very delicate, and leapt to the ceiling
like Fred Astaire.
   I was in London last week, and read some poems to night-
students of the university. I didn't like the people at all; some
looked like lemons, and all spoke with the voices of puddings.
I detest the humility I should have, and am angry when I am
humble. I appreciate the social arrogance I have in the face of
my humility. . . . I bow before ——, seeing the family likeness
in the old familiar faeces, but I will not manure the genealogi-
cal tree . . . Your poems, Ballad, Mana, Griefs, Sunset, were
more successful—from the point of controversy afterwards—

35

than any I read. By a few, your poems in "Wales" have been admired: The Sunbather, in particular, got them on their backs. Will you send me any new poems there are? I shall probably be addressing, from my canonical chair, more earnest suckers next month; & I'd prefer them to suck up something valuable.

I've been writing some poems, but they're away, in the house of an enemy, being typed. They're matter-of-fact poems, & illogical naturally: except by a process it's too naturally obvious to misexplain. Rhymes are coming to me naturally, too, which I distrust; I like looking for connections, not finding them tabulated in stations. A sense of humour is, I hope, about to be lost: but not quite yet: the self-drama continues: bluff after bluff until I see myself as one: then again the deadly humour. But don't bother about this understated difficulty. Send me poems, & I'll send you some. Mine—not through humility or knowledge of less competence—will be more unsatisfactory. At the moment I am, in action, a person of words, & not as I should be: a person of words in action.

Here's a photograph, taken by a woman near us. It's one of many: this is the toughest. Why I want you to think of me,—photographically, when I'm not about—as a tough, I don't know. Anyway, it's very big; you can write a poem on the back, draw whiskers on it, or advertize Kensitas in the front window.

My love to you, my regards to your family, & write soon. I hope to see you before the summer. Caitlin is well, happy, & dancing. I miss you.   DYLAN.

The next letter refers in its third paragraph to a phrase in my poem 'Thames Forest' which I had shown him when we first met:

> Of all forms living man alone deliberate
> Scrawls on a leaf the impression of his going.
> These leaves are numbered.

The long poem referred to at the end of this letter is 'How Shall
My Animal'. *The three short ones are* 'O Make Me a Mask
and a Wall to Shut from Your Spies', 'Not From This Anger',
and the first part of the poem 'In Memory of Ann Jones'.

The poems of mine discussed in paragraph two of the letter are
'Call It All Names, But Do Not Call It Rest', *an early draft of
the poem with a different title being all I had then written of it:*
'The Windows'; *and* 'The Collier'. *The first of these was printed
in* Poetry (Chicago) *in October 1952; the other two in* Ballad of
the Mari Lwyd & Other Poems, 'The Windows' *being afterwards revised under the title* 'The Eastern Window' *for the
second edition.*

[*Undated: envelope dated 21st March 1938*]
Blashford, Ringwood, Hants.

Dear Vernon,

Many thanks for your letter, and for the poems before. We
are not going to Ireland, and we will try to be in Gower some
time in the summer. The reason I haven't written for such a
time is not because I found nothing to say about your new
poems, but because I have been in London, in penury, and in
doubt: In London, because money lives and breeds there; in
penury, because it doesn't; and in doubt as to whether I should
continue as an outlaw or take my fate for a walk in the straight
and bowler-treed paths. The conceit of outlaws is a wonderful
thing; they think they can join the ranks of regularly-conducted
society whenever they like. You hear young artists talk glibly
about, "God, I've a good mind to chuck this perilous, unsatisfactory, moniless business of art and go into the City & make
money". But who wants them in the City? If you are a
money-&-success-maker, you make it in whatever you do. And
young artists are always annoyed and indignant if they hear a
City-man say, "God, I've a good mind to chuck this safe,
monotonous business of money-making & go into the wilder-
ness and make poems".

Poems. I liked the three you sent me. There is something

very unsatisfactory, though, about "All mists, all thoughts" which seems—using the vaguest words—to lack a central strength. All the words are lovely, but they *seem* so *chosen*, not struck out. I can see the sensitive picking of words, but none of the strong, inevitable pulling that makes a poem an event, a happening, an action perhaps, not a still-life or an experience put down, placed, regulated; the introduction of mist, legend, time's weir, grief's bell, & such things as "which held, but knew not her", the whole of the 13th line, "all griefs that we suppose", seem to me "literary", not living. They seem, as indeed the whole poem seems, to come out of the nostalgia of literature; the growth is not, like, say, Rossetti's, a hothouse growth, but one that has been seeded from a flower placed, long ago in the smelling and blowing and growing past, between pages. A motive has been rarefied, it should be made common. I don't ask you for vulgarity, though I miss it; I think I ask you for a little creative destruction, destructive creation: "I build a flying tower, and I pull it down". Neither —a phrase we used once, do you remember?—could I call this an 'indoor' poem; one doesn't need the sun in a poem to make it hot. But—though this [is] silly—it is a poem so obviously written in words; I want my sentimental blood: not Roy Campbell's blood, which is a red & noisy adjective in a transparent vein, but the blood of leaves, wells, weirs, fonts, shells, echoes, rainbows, olives, bells, oracles, sorrows. Of course I can't explain my feelings about the poem, except, sentimentally speaking again, to say that I want a poem to do more than just to have the appearance of 'having been created'. I think, of the poem, that the words are chosen, & then lie down contented with your choice.

"Was that a grief" has a lot more vulgarity in it, breaches of the nostalgic etiquette. There are, too, I think, stalenesses: "a later threnody", "in the years to be"; awkwardnesses: "Next from blood's side, with poppy's nonchalance"; weaknesses: "Their fingers frail as tendrils of light's flower". Stale, because the words come, not quite without thinking, but with-

38

out fresh imagining: down they go, the germ of what you want & what is yours ready-folded in a phrase not yours and that you don't need. The awkwardness of "poppy's nonchalance" is obvious: it sounds like a man with a lisp & a stutter trying to gargle. And weak, because that particular alliterative line is too easily-taken, a "breather-between" energies. But I like the poem greatly, your 'grand lines' in the 4th verse are as grand as they could be. And all of it has your own peculiar power of minute concentration: the immense, momentous scrawl on the leaf.

I've always liked your ballads very much, & so far—inevitably—the ballads & lyrics mean more to me than the long & complicated poems. Will you let me send the Collier ballad to Robert Herring?

Here are 4 poems, two short simple ones, done fairly quickly, a conventional sonnet, and one I have spent a great deal of time on. The typewriter I generally use has been taken from me. Could you type these out for me? I very much want to send them away some-time at the end of this week and sell them for a mouse's ransom.

I haven't finished the World* story yet, but I'm working on a series of short, straightforward stories about Swansea. One has been finished & published, & I'll send you a copy when I have one: which will [be] in a few days.

Don't be too harsh to these poems until they're typed; I always think typescript lends some sort of certainty: at least, if the things are bad then, they appear to be bad with conviction; in ordinary mss. they look as though they might be altered at any moment.

Write soon and send a poem.

Love,
DYLAN.

PS. About "blowing" light in the last verse. Can you think of anything better? Do try.

*'In the Direction of the Beginning.'

In answering his last letter I had called the long poem 'How Shall My Animal' an 'opus' and the shorter three 'opossums', just to make it easy to refer to them.

The third paragraph is again dealing with my poem, 'The Windows'. He did use the youthfully-made phrase 'When I woke the dawn spoke' (written in a schoolboy's notebook and probably composed before he was fifteen) much later in a Deaths and Entrances *poem where it became:*

> When I woke
> The town spoke.

Blashford, Ringwood, Hants., April 1, 38.

Dear V:

The mouse is released, the cheesy bandits have nibbled off, there are squeaks of jubilation, and whiskers glint in the sun. Thank you very much indeed for the present; it came when we had no tubular white ants to smoke, when we needed them passionately; now we've got antheaps, and this evening we go to the pictures, and your closeup shall be brighter than any.

I liked your two words, and am keeping both. I'm as sure now as you are of the 'lionhead', and 'whinnying' is certainly far better than my word and may—I am coming to think it is—be the best. I'm so glad you liked the poem, I had worked on it for months. The opossums are unsatisfactory, I know. Before your letter came, I had cut out the ubiquitous 'weather' from the anticlimatic poem, and am revising it all; I will conquer "rebellion in"; and 'eyed' tongue shall, momentarily, become 'lashed'. The poem in memory of Anne Jones I am completely rewriting; and again the 'weather' shall drop out: I'm making it longer and, I hope, better than any of my recent simple poems.

In one thing you are still wrong: 'poppy's nonchalance' is bad; it cannot be anything *but* bad; and I refute your criticism from the bottom of my catarrh. "In the years to be" should, of course, stand; I was silly, and perhaps priggish, to call it a

40

catchphrase; there is no reason why it shouldn't be and no reason that you should not revitalize it if it were; I've got one of those very youthfully-made phrases, too, that often comes to my mind & which one day I shall use: "When I woke, the dawn spoke". You are right to write poems of all kinds; I only write poems of allsorts, and, like the Liquorice sweets, they all taste the same.

I've just read a poem in an American paper, that I think's very good: Evening Prayer:*

> with these O God these
> sins of the light prayers were
> reserved for sleep
>
> forehead of childhood
> and the dark take care
> take all your sight inside

blanket
> night night the blankets grave
> the smell of blanket breathing
> sleep dimness the beasts
>
> come soft shaken and the eyes
> across nothing like air
> O God my words in darkness
>
> to be warm to be brave to
> go packed in armour rising
> sometimes in air

stoneweary knees
> stone weary knees
> and to you father
sleep sleep sleep sleep
> sleep sleep sleep

* This poem is by Robert Fitzgerald, from 'A Wreath for the Sea', now collected in the volume *In the Rose of Time* (New Directions 1956). Differences between the text in the letter and the printed text are indicated in the margin.

grass and lilac and   grass & lilac &
through my most grievous fault
the beast is unappeased

the agony in the garden
now I unclasp my hands
into thy hands my spirit.

_____

I'm looking forward very much to seeing you.
And thanks again,
Love, DYLAN.
& CAITLIN.

[*See page 57*]

Dylan had spent three months staying with his parents at Bishopston, within three miles of my home. We had seen a great deal of each other during that time. He was now living in Laugharne.

The Auden appreciation, mentioned in the next letter, had been printed in the Auden Double Number of New Verse *edited by Geoffrey Grigson, for which a number of appreciations from various writers had been collected. To Dylan's own contribution, which was one of sincere praise, he added a postscript: 'Congratulations on Auden's seventieth birthday.'*

Gosport St., Laugharne, Carms., 5th July 1938

Dear Vernon,
When are you and Francis, or you or Francis, coming here again? Come soon. My mother wrote to tell me that she'd seen you, & that you told her you hoped we weren't too tired when you arrived that Sunday. Of course we weren't. It's always lovely to see you. I've nearly finished my story,* & you must see it & read it in detail & tell me where I am too extravagant.
Harvard University wrote to ask me for something for their

* 'One Warm Saturday.'

42

special magazine in honour of Eliot—just a paragraph or two of what I think of him, his writing, his religion, his influence, etc. I've written a heap of notes, none of which seems really satisfactory. Do please tell me a few things, just as you helped with that little Auden appreciation. Just a few comments or notes.

Don't forget to come soon.

Love,

DYLAN.

Wednesday: [*envelope dated 14th July, 1938*]
Gosport St., Laugharne

Dear Vernon,

We'll be able to come up to Bishopston this weekend. Is Francis coming here on Thursday? We've had no word yet. News when we meet. Think about Eliot for me. Are you listening-in tonight?

Love,

DYLAN.

The ballad-like poem sent with the next letter was 'The Tombstone Told When She Died'. 'Great' was afterwards altered to 'dear' in the last line, as shown in the letter following.

The second poem which accompanied the letter was, almost certainly, 'On No Work Of Words Now'.

Sunday [*probably September 1938*]
Sea View, Laugharne, Carmarthenshire

Dear Vernon,

Thanks for the letter & the poem which I like immensely now, after many readings; it's one of the very best, & I'll write more about it soon to you (& about 2 others I've got) or read it over with you when we meet.

Here are 2 short ones of mine, just done. Could you type them properly for me? In the ballad-like poem I'm not *quite*

43

sure of several words, mostly of "great" floods of his hair. I think it's right, though; I didn't want a surprisingly strong word there. Do tell me about it, soon.

What about a weekend here? There's plenty of food, beds, & welcome. Come by bike. What about next weekend? Let me know.

Love,

D.

The poems 'The Tombstone Told When She Died' and 'A Saint About To Fall' accompanied the next letter, and its two paragraphs are concerned with them in that order. The second poem, on which he had been working continuously, was written in anticipation of the birth of his first child in January.

The postscript about OGRE refers to the poem 'On No Work Of Words Now' which I had typed and sent back to him.

Monday: [*sent 14th October 1938*], *Sea View, Laugharne.*
Dear Vernon,

I'm sorry not to have written before, I've been awfully busy with my own work, with reviewing, & muddled up with trying to get money from a sinister philanthropic society. Here's my new big poem and—with no anger at all—the Hardy-like one. I considered all your suggestions most carefully. A 'strange & red' harsh head was, of course, very weak & clumsy, but I couldn't see that the alliteration of "raving red" was effective. I tried everything, & stuck to the commonplace "blazing", which makes the line violent enough then, if not exactly good enough, for the last. In the last line you'll see I've been daring, & have tried to make the point of the poem softer & subtler by the use of the dangerous "dear". The word "dear" fits in, I think, with "though her eyes smiled", which comes earlier. I wanted the girl's *terrible* reaction to orgastic [sic] death to be suddenly altered into a kind of despairing love. As I see it now, it strikes me as very moving, but it may be too much of a

44

shock, a bathetic shock perhaps, & I'd like very much to know what you think. No, I still think the womb "bellowing" is allright, exactly what I wanted; perhaps it looks too much like a stunt rhyme with heroine, but that was unavoidable. "Hurried" film I just couldn't see; I wanted it slow & complicated, the winding cinematic works of the womb. I agree with your objection to "small"; "innocent" is splendid, but "fugitive" & "turbulent" are, for me in that context, too vague, too 'literary' (I'm sorry to use that word again) too ambiguous. I've used "devilish", which is almost colloquial.

As to the big poem—only provisionally called "In September", & called that at all only because it was a terrible war month—I'm at the moment very pleased with it, more than with anything I've done this year. Does "Glory cracked like a flea" shock you? I think you'll see it *must* come there, or some equally grotesque contrast. The last line of the 2nd verse might appear just a long jumble of my old anatomical cliches, but if, in the past, I've used "burning brains & hair" etc too loosely, this time I used them—as the only words—in dead earnest. Remember this is a poem written to a child about to be born—you know I'm going to be a father in January—& telling it what a world it will see, what horrors & hells. The last four lines of the poem, especially the last but two, may seem ragged, but I've altered the rhythm purposely; "you so gentle" must be very soft and gentle, & the last line must roar. It's an optimistic, taking-everything, poem. The two most important words are "Cry Joy". Tell me about this, please, very soon. I'm surer of the *words* of this poem than of the words in any recent one. I want mostly to know what the general effect of the poem is upon you (though of course you can criticize, as you like, any detail).

Sorry you couldn't come this weekend. Do try to come next. I'm afraid we're much too poor to be able to come up to see you for a long time. So do your best.

All Love,
DYLAN.

The following typed quatrain was sent on a separate sheet of paper with this letter: it was printed that winter in the magazine Seven:

I, the first named, am the ghost of this sir and Christian friend
Who writes these words I write in a still room in a spellsoaked house:
I am the ghost in this house that is filled with the tongue and eyes
Of a lack-a-head ghost I fear to the anonymous end.

[*On reverse of envelope:*]
Can you send me a typed copy of the long poem?
The word is OGRE, not orge or orgy &, as Pritchard [sic] would say, I'll listen to no criticisms of it.

I had sent Dylan a free, rhymed translation of Novalis's hymn, 'Wenn Alle Untreu Werden'.

The poem referred to in the next letter's second paragraph is 'A Saint About To Fall'; the story, one of those for Portrait Of The Artist As a Young Dog, *many of which were printed first in* Life and Letters.

Saturday: [*sent 19th October 1938*]
Sea View, Laugharne, Carmarthenshire

Dear Vernon,
I'm going to Manchester on Tuesday to take part in a programme, that will be broadcast on the National, sweetly called the Modern Muse. About 10.30 at night. Don't forget to listen in. I'll probably read one, at the most two, short poems of my own, &, for that alone, the journey wouldn't be worth while; but I may as well go up to meet Auden, Spender, Macneice, Day-Lewis & some others who'll be there; Minnie Roberts is compereing, which is just about his job. I'll tell you all about

46

it in Swansea, for I'll come back there on Wednesday. Looking forward to seeing you.

Thank you for typing the poems, & for the things you said. I agree that 'carbolic' & 'strike' cd be bettered, but, at the moment, I'll just leave them; I may be able to go back clearly to the poem some time soon, but I'll publish it now as it is in Life & Letters, & then we'll see. Glad you liked the straight story; I'm doing another now: illuminated reporting.

That hymn must be great in the original, I wish I could read German.

Love,

DYLAN

I cannot describe my excitement when I saw for the first time on a postcard the poem for his twenty-fourth birthday which Dylan Thomas afterwards printed at the end of The Map of Love. *It was surrounded by commentary, in his minute writing, which is clear enough except in its reference to the last line. A year or two before, Dylan had read me an unfinished poem, based on images of hunting, which had opened with the line:*

For as long as forever is,

and which was divided into separate verses of which he had finished, I think, either two or three. The last line of the first verse had been:

Forever the hunted world at a snail's gallop goes.

I agreed with all the commentary. My only disagreement turned on the bracketed second line of the poem.

Postcard sent from Laugharne on 24th October 1938

BIRTHDAY POEM

Twenty four years remind the tears of my eyes.
(Bury the dead for fear that they walk to the grave in labour).

In the groin of the natural doorway I crouched like a tailor
Sewing a shroud for a journey
By the light of the meat-eating sun.
Dressed to die, the sensual strut begun,
With my red veins full of money,
In the final direction of the elementary town
I advance for as long as forever is.

———

[note at side:] This poem's just a statement,
perhaps.

This very short poem is for my birthday just arriving. I know
you'll hate the use of the "Forever" line, but there it is. I
scrapped the poem beginning with that line long ago, and at
last—I think—I've found the inevitable place for it: it was a
time finding that place. I'm pleased, terribly, with this—so far.
Do tell me, & type please. In the first version I had "like a
stuffed tailor". I think stuffed is wrong, don't you? Try to
read the end of the poem as though you didn't know the lines.
I do feel they're right. In the old "Forever" poem they were
completely out of place—& the rest of the poem wouldn't
stand without them. So bang went the whole poem, obviously,
& here at last is what it should be.

*The next three letters come from Ringwood where Dylan and
Caitlin were now staying in expectation of the birth of their child.
'Poem in the Ninth Month', the title I suggested for 'A Saint
about to Fall', was used in* Poetry (London), *where this poem was
first printed, but not in* The Map of Love *where, as in the*
Collected Poems, *the first line was used as title.*

*I had told Dylan about the way Malherbe used to letter his
underpants, and how he once astonished Racan by saying that he
was 'wearing up to L'.*

The story 'In the Direction of the Beginning' remained a frag-

48

ment. First printed in Wales, *it was posthumously collected in the book entitled* A Prospect of the Sea.

Blashford, Ringwood, Hants., December 20, 1938

Dear Vernon,

It's almost too cold to hold a pen this morning. I've lost a toe since breakfast, my nose is on its last nostril. I've four sweaters on (including yours), two pairs of trousers & socks, a leather coat & a dressing-gown. Who was the French poet who had alphabetically lettered underpants, & wore every one up to H on a cold morning?

I've just come back from three dark days in London, city of the restless dead. It really is an insane city, & filled me with terror. Every pavement drills through your soles to your scalp, and out pops a lamp-post covered with hair. I'm not going to London again for years; its intelligentsia is so hurried in the head that nothing stays there; its glamour smells of goat; there's no difference between good & bad.

I went to see Dent's—Church, really—about a new book. I'm making it an odd book: 15 poems & 5 stories: all to be called In the Direction Of The Beginning. It may look a mess, but I hope not.

It was a great pity we didn't manage to get down to Bishopston before coming here for Christmas and birth; it's been a long time since seeing you, and I want your new poems. Please write quickly, *for* Christmas, with them & news. I'm enclosing a little new poem; been doing several little ones lately; send you them all soon.

Thank you for "Poem In the Ninth Month". It's fine. I'll use it, of course. And sorry about that bracketed line in the birthday poem, but, until I can think of something else or feel, it will have to stay. I thought your alternative line clumsier & more bass-drum (rather muffled, too) than mine. I do realise your objections to my line; I feel myself the too selfconscious flourish, recognize the Shakespeare echo (though echo's not the word). If ever I do alter it, I'll *remember* your line.

Was the American anthology you mentioned one edited by Norman McCaig? I've sent him something. Will you let me see the revised "Room of Pity". And the Yeats poem, please.

This morning the secretary of the London Verse-Speaking Choir—I think it was called—rang me up & asked me whether I could attend the final rehearsal before making an H.M.V. record, of their speaking of my "And Death Shall Have No D". I said I couldn't, so there & then the Choir recited it to me down the telephone. Oh dear. Picked voices picking the rhythm to bits, chosen elocutionists choosing their own meanings, ten virgins weeping slowly over a quick line, matrons mooing the refrain, a conductor with all his vowels planed to the last e.

Caitlin's very strong & well & full. She sends love. So do I, as you know. My silence is never sulks. Remember me to your father & mother. Regards to Dot & Marjorie. Have the best Christmas.

Last year at this time Caitlin & I were doing an act in a garret. This time we're just as poor, or poorer, but the ravens —soft, white, silly ravens—will feed us.

Yes, I wish I was in Swansea sometimes too.

Ever,

DYLAN.

We've got a Monopoly set. Apparently the Monopoly manufacturers have made a new game, called—I think— Families. It's all to do with ages, & the point is not to die.

Contemporary Poetry and Prose *was edited by Roger Rough-ton. He stayed with Dylan at Laugharne and was on friendly terms with him. When Roughton died tragically during the war Dylan told me that his own address was one of two found in his pockets.*

The Yeats poem mentioned in the next letter is ' Yeats in Dublin', printed in Life and Letters *in April 1939, and collected, after some rewriting, in my second book,* The Lamp And The Veil.

Blashford, Ringwood, Hants., 29 December, 1938

Dear Vernon,

What a lovely Compendium. We play all the games in turn. Halma is a demon's game, but one called Winkle's Wedding is too young and sounds like a mass-poem written by adolescents in Roughton's dead paper. Did Families exist? I had a stocking this year, full of sweets and cigars and mouthorgans and cherry brandy. Thank you also for the pretty croquet card. I wish there was something to send you, apart from my love & the small poem I forgot to enclose last time. Before I forget: there's a new periodical, Poetry (London) which promises to be, if nothing else, well produced. A monthly. Edited by man or woman called Tambimuttu. Contributors, God bless them, to the first number will have their names engraved on the special souvenir cover. Will you send it something? It may be honest; if so, it shouldn't want to pack its pages with the known stuff of the known boys; a new paper should give —(say)—Barker a rest: he must be very tired. The address of Tambimuttu is 114 Whitfield St, London. W.1.

Is Fig still with you, and how was your holiday? Ours was long and weakening, with parties, charades, and too much. Now we reform again; I have a study with the door compulsorily locked and no thrillers allowed inside; there'll be nothing to do but poems.

Congratulations on the magnificent Yeats poem: so few faults in such noble danger; the fine feeling constant. That may be smug to say, but I'm sick of avoiding cliches of appreciation & expressing a large like in small, tough terms. I think it's one of your most truly felt poems; that's not to say that other poems of yours are not true or felt, but only to say that the purity in it is never less than the poetry. What a poem for the old man after that historic interview. In another letter later I'll tell you the few things in the poem that are, to me, uneffectively understated: one or two instances, especially in the reported speech, when understatement is an excess & moderation, economical sobriety, a wallow. But now I want only to tell you how moved I was by the poem, & how much I admire it.

This is quick thanks. My little news must come with my Yeats' grumbles.

Write soon.

DYLAN.

Caitlin sends her love, too, to all of you.

POEM

Once it was the colour of saying
Soaked my table the uglier side of a hill
With a capsized field where a school sat still
And a black and white patch of girls grew playing;
The seaslides of saying I must undo
That all the charmingly dead arise to cockcrow & kill.
When I whistled with mitching boys through a reservoir park
Where we stoned at night the close and cuckoo
Lovers in the dirt of their leafy beds,
The shade of their trees was a word of many shades
And a lamp of lightning for the poor in the dark;
Now my saying shall be my undoing
And every stone I wind off like a reel.

This Cwmdonkin poem—minus pandemonium*—*must*, please, be typed before read. Don't send me a copy. I've got one. There's a fullstop after "kill" in the 6th line.

* 'minus pandemonium' refers to a line of my poem in memory of Pearl White:

'Of Pandemonium near Cwmdonkin Park'

John Prichard, whose name is incorrectly spelt at the beginning of the next letter, was in pre-war days one of the circle of friends who met at the Kardomah in Swansea every week. He contributed poems and short stories to Wales *and is well represented in Keidrych Rhys's Faber anthology,* Modern Welsh Poetry.

The poem referred to in the third paragraph of the next letter is ' Once It Was The Colour Of Saying '.

Francis Dufau-Labeyrie, besides translating the book, Portrait Of The Artist As A Young Dog, *into French, also translated several of the earlier stories including ' A Prospect Of The Sea' which was printed in* L'Arche.

Sunday [January 1939: postmark 8/1/39]
Blashford, Ringwood, Hants.

Dear Vernon,

I was told you telephoned. Caitlin and I didn't get back until fairly late, and as you said it wasn't a call of life & death we took you at your word and didn't worry. I'll ring you one night. It will be nice to hear you again, those soft Cambridge accents sliding from Wales. Thank you.

Since you've apparently been taking lessons from John Pritchard [sic] in refusing to accept adverse criticism, I shall make my grumbles about your good Yeats poem illegible to invisibility. Here come the grumbles, hot, strong, and logical, but you can't see them. Incidentally, the effectiveness of a history of conversation is determined by selection. Though the statements are word for word, the words are still wrong in the poem. You can say to me that effectiveness is less than truth; I can only say that the truth must be made effectively true, and though every word of the truth be put down the result may well be a clot of *truths.*

I'm glad you like my last poem. I shan't alter anything in it except, perhaps, but probably, the 'close & cuckoo' lovers. The 'dear close cuckoo' lovers is a good suggestion. I can't say

53

the same for 'halo for the bruised knee and broken heel' which is esoterically *off* every mark in the poem. I see your argument about the error of shape, but the form was consistently emotional and I can't change it without a change of heart.

Last week I went up to London to meet Henry Miller who is a dear, mad, mild man, bald and fifty, with great enthusiasms for commonplaces. Also Lawrence Durrell. We spent 2 days together, and I returned a convinced wreck. We talked our way through the shabby saloons of nightmare London. I saw, too, Cameron who has written a good poem, —— —— who has no merit, & a man dressed in brown paper.

We shall play with the Compendium, & are now the very disappointed owners of bran-new Milestones which is a kiddies' mixture of Ludo & Happy Families & quite without the subversive, serious charm of Monopoly. A woman bought the set for us, so it really was lucky you didn't.

I'll tell you when the great birthday comes. We're waiting now. Caitlin had very few angles before, but now she has none. The word is mellow.

We'll be back in Wales, I hope, at the end of February. Certainly in March. Laugharne will be beautiful in the Spring. You must come often. We'll learn, perhaps, to sail together. Love to your family, &, of course, to yourself.

DYLAN.

I'll write a better letter soon, with a poem.
But you must write too.
Do you know which stories of mine Francis has translated? A chap called Constantine Fitzgibbon—you saw his translation of a little poem in "La Nouvelle Saison"—wants to do my "Lemon" story. Is Francis doing that?

Yeats died on January 28th, 1939; Llewelyn Thomas was born two days later.

54

Blashford, Ringwood, Hants., 1 February 1939.

Dear Vernon,

This is just to tell you that Caitlin & I have a son aged 48 hours. Its name is Llewelyn Thomas. It is red-faced, very angry, & blue-eyed. Bit blue, bit green. It does not like the world. Caitlin is well, & beautiful. I'm sorry Yeats is dead. What a loss of the great poems he would write. Aged 73, he died in his prime. Caitlin's address—if you would like to send her a word—is Maternity Ward, Cornelia Hospital, Poole, Dorset.

Our love to you,

DYLAN.

[Pencil letter from Caitlin Thomas]
Cornelia Hospital, Poole, 4th February 1939

Dear Vernon,

It was kind of you to write. I think Llewelyn is the better name, he is a very intriguing person, you must give your opinion on his head bumps, his head is long and fibrous, & his face squashed red & angry like Dylan—

Will you thank your mother & father for their good wishes, and by the way I never told you how pleased I was about the wireless you got for us. I hope we can manage to connect it, it will be lovely.

We hope to be back in Wales soon & see you all—I am sick of this old England.

It is marvellous to have shed my burden at last! love to you and yours.

CAITLIN

Blashford, Ringwood, Hants., Saturday [February, 1939]

Dear Vernon,

A very short letter to thank you for your letters to Caitlin and me about our mumbling boy. He's in the room with me now, making noises to his fingers, his eyes unfocusing, with his red skull half-covered in golden cotton. He & Caitlin came back from hospital today. She's well.

55

Here's a new poem. Tell me: is it too short? do I end before the point? does it need more room to work to a meaning, any expansion? I intended it as a longer & more ambitious thing, but stopped it suddenly thinking it was complete. How do you feel about it? And what about a poem from you? Write very soon.

Ever yours,
DYLAN.

Have you ever seen such insulting rot as that written about Yeats in the respectable Sunday newspapers.

[Enclosure:]

January 1939

Because the pleasure-bird whistles after the hot wires,
Shall the blind horse sing sweeter?
Convenient bird and beast lie lodged to suffer
The supper and knives of a mood.
In the sniffed and poured snow on the tip of the tongue of the
    year
That clouts the spittle like bubbles with broken rooms,
An enamoured man alone with the twigs of his eyes, two fires,
Camped in the drug-white shower of nerves and food,
Savours the lick of the times through a deadly wood of hair
In a wind that plucked a goose,
Nor ever, as the wild tongue breaks its tombs,
Rounds to look at the red, wagged root.
Because there stands, one story out of the bum city,
That frozen wife whose juices drift like a fixed sea
Secretly in statuary,
Shall I, struck on the hot and rocking street,
Not spin to stare at an old year
Toppling and burning in the muddle of towers and galleries
Like the mauled pictures of boys?
The salt person and blasted place
I furnish with the meat of a fable.

If the dead starve, their stomachs turn to tumble
An upright man in the antipodes
Or spray-based and rock-chested sea:
Over the past table I repeat this present grace.

(Note:) The word is CHESTED.

*The poem in memory of Ann Jones had been sent me in a much
shorter form with the letter on page 37. It had consisted simply
of the first fifteen lines, ending with:*

Round the parched worlds of Wales and drowned each sun.

*The bracketed lines were then added, and the rest of the poem
came 'in a rush'. The completed version that accompanied this
letter had important differences from the final text, the chief being
that 'gesture and psalm' in line 37 were used as verbs, greatly
weakening line 38, about which he felt uncertain. The poem was
printed in* Life and Letters *(Summer, 1938). So it is clear
that I have been deceived by the envelope and that this letter
belongs to page 42.*

*'Broken Net' was the early version of my 'Ballad Of Dundrum
Bay', published in* Life and Letters *during the war, but not
yet collected in a book.*

[No date: envelope dated February 1939]
Blashford, Ringwood, Hants.

Dear Vernon,
    In haste. Thank you for the letter & the revised poem; I
shall write tomorrow evening—so that perhaps our letters
cross—about this & the Broken Net. Now here is the Anne
Jones poem, & now I think it is more of a poem; will you
type it for me? I knew it was feeble as it stood before, & the
end of it—that is the part that becomes the new brackets—was
too facile &, almost, grandiosely sentimental. (By the way,
when you type it, will you spell Anne as Ann: I just remember

that's the right way: she was an ancient peasant aunt) I think there are some good lines, but don't know abt the thing as a whole.

News—I have a little—& criticisms etc in tomorrow's long letter. You don't mind typing for me, do you? I'm looking forward to what you say about the poem. But—again—don't read it till it's typed.

The 38th line may seem weak, but I think I wanted it like that. Anyway. . . .

Love to you
DYLAN

Wednesday: [envelope dated 3rd March 1939]
Blashford, Ringwood, Hants.

Dear Vernon,

Very short note. I've got to do the proofs of my new book of poems this week, & I'm thinking of putting in this poem just finished. Please, can I have a quick criticism. It's deeply felt, but perhaps clumsily said. In particular—is the last line too bad, too comic, or does it *just* work? Have you any alternatives for the *adjectives* of that last line?—you see obviously what I *mean*.

Terrific hurry to get this in time for post.

Hope you're well. Back in a fortnight. Letter much sooner. Caitlin & Llewelyn well. Hope you are.

My love,
DYLAN.

[Enclosed with letter:]

POEM

" If my head hurt a hair's foot
Pack back the downed bone. If the unpricked ball of my breath
Bump on a spout let the bubbles jump out.
Sooner drop with the worm of the ropes round my throat
Than bully ill love in the clouted scene.

58

All game phrases fit your ring of a cockfight:
I'll comb the snared woods with a glove on a lamp.
Peck, sprint, dance on fountains, and duck time
Before I rush in a crouch the ghost with a hammer, air,
Strike light, and bloody a loud room.

If my bunched, monkey coming is cruel
Rage me back to the making house. My hand unravel
When you sew the deep door. The bed is a cross place.
Bend, if my journey ache, direction like an arc or make
A limp and riderless shape to leap nine thinning months."

"No. Not for Christ's dazzling bed
Or a nacreous sleep among soft particles and charms
My dear would I change my tears or your iron head.
Thrust, my daughter or son, to escape there is none, none, none
Nor when all ponderous heaven's host of waters breaks.

Now to awake husked of gestures and my calm like a cave
To the anguish and carrion, to the infant forever unfree,
O my lost love bounced from a good home.
The grain that hurries this way from the rim of the grave
Has a voice and a house: there and here you must couch and
    cry.

Rest beyond choice in the dust-appointed grain,
At the breast stored with seas. No return
Through the waves of the fat streets nor the skeleton's thin
    ways.
The grave and my calm body are shut to your coming as stone,
And the endless, tremendous beginning suffers open".

Blashford, Ringwood, Hants.

Dear Vernon,

I didn't write sooner because I thought I'd be returning. Now I know it'll be April 6 or 7 when we drive back to the best places. We'll be in Bishopston one day at Easter, the boy with us.

I agreed with every word you wrote abt my poem. The 2nd person speaks better than the first, & the last line is false. I haven't been able to alter the first part, & will have to leave it unsuccessful. The last line is now: "And the endless beginning of prodigies suffers open". I worked on from your suggestion.

I'd like to go over the final proofs of all the poems with you, but that won't be for a few weeks. Some weeks. Did I tell you the book,* which will be priced at 7/6 and have a John frontispiece portrait, includes 7 s. stories as well. All unviolent ones. Church refused to pass the best, "P. of the Sea" because of its "unwarrantable moments of sensuality"—the fish. Perhaps I'll make a little money from this book: I think a lot of 'readers' prefer to pay 7/6 for a book to 3/6.

Does Dot know Lawrence's "Kangaroo" poem? Send her my love. The favourite meal in Australia—"The Ritz couldn't do you better my boy" an Australian told a man I know when he was out there—is a very underdone steak with an over-poached egg on top, followed by a cup of tea.

News when we meet. Quite a lot too.

Love from us,
DYLAN.

Laugharne

I was too late for the shops in Swansea
I couldn't get a Life & Letters. I shall in Carmarthen tomorrow. Is there any other good news?

Laugharne is, I've found out,
D.C.

Dear Vernon,

Godfather by proxy you shall be, and I'm very glad you can be. As to a gift: honestly don't worry about that, we've just had a big gift from you. Is the wireless set, please, A.C. or D.C.? The expert here can't tell & daren't test it until he knows for certain; he might blow it up. It was grand to see you, and you must come down soon, a very soon weekend. Until today it's been wonderful here, & we've driven all about Carmarthenshire in the large car you saw. We're still, of course, without a penny. I'll bring the last batch of proofs to you as soon as they come; or you spend a critical day with them here. We were sorry to miss your mother. Don't forget about the wireless.

Love,
DYLAN.
& from CAITLIN & LLEWELYN.

I had met Robert Herring, Editor of Life *and* Letters *in London, on my way back from a short holiday in Paris. Dylan had returned to Laugharne the previous month.*

The poem referred to in the next two letters is 'When all my five and country senses see.'

Laugharne

I'm sending this to your office
because I've got the idea,
wrong perhaps, that you leave
before the first post arrives.

Dear Vernon,

Glad you're back from Paris. Waiting to hear everything. Herring wrote me & told me you'd been to see him. Impression?

* *The Map of Love*
61

Proofs of my poems just come. One poem I want to rewrite *with* your assistance; but I must do it quickly. Can you come down Saturday—for, if possible, the weekend? Please try, I need your help a lot. It really is important to me.

this Saturday, 13th, of course.

Love from us all,

DYLAN.

P.T.O.

Bring your masque. Herring wants me to write about it for the July number.

We haven't had the wireless set up in our house yet. It's still in Billy Williams's—he's the local electrician. He wanted me to get hold of the set's book of instructions for him, or, at any rate, a little 3 plug lead which is supposed to go in at the back of the machine but which wasn't among the parts you gave me. Billy says the set, *without* this little plug thing, will go beautifully in the day-time but makes a bad noise as soon as the Laugharne electric power is started. The plug thing will cut out the bad noise. I meant to ask you about this before, but you were away.

[*No date: envelope 12th May 1939*], *Laugharne.*

Dear Vernon,

I don't know if you leave Pennard before the first post comes or not. In case you do, there's a note from me waiting you in your Bank. This is an extra note—because if, & I hope terribly that you can, you do come, you might want to let your people know *not* by telephone alone, & get a few things, pyjamas perhaps. By 'come' I mean come to Laugharne—as the other note will tell you. I need you urgently to rewrite a poem with me that belongs to the final proofs of my book which have to be sent off almost at once.

Love,

DYLAN.

Dylan was now seeing a great deal of the author Richard Hughes, who owned Laugharne Castle. In a contributor's note he had written in Life *and* Letters *about Laugharne: ' Its literary values are firmly established: Richard Hughes lives in a castle at the top of the hill; I live in a shed at the bottom.'*

In the poem which came with the next letter, I did, as he anticipated, object to the last line. I thought it let the poem down.

[*Undated: probably May 1939*], *Sea View, Laugharne*

Dear Vernon,

I don't think I ever wrote to you after you sent the magazine with your Yeats poem in it. Sorry. I liked the poem, of course, and it seemed more closely worked than what I remember the first version to have been. Hughes & I read it together.

Here's my new poem. I hope you'll think it's good; I'm extremely pleased with it at the moment—it was written in a very enjoyable mood, (or any other better word) of surly but optimistic passion—though it is, as you'll see, in places a little awkward. I am not sure of the word "animal" in the last line but one of the first stanza; it says more or less what I mean, that the rails, the frame if you like, of the bed of the grave is living, sensual, serpentine, but it's a word I've used perhaps too often.

"Crotch"—last line, third stanza—I've also used, once fairly startlingly, but I'm afraid the word is quite essential here. Or so, at the moment, I think. The last two lines I can see you disliking, especially the crude last lump. But that sudden crudeness is (again) essential to the argument, to, if you don't mind, the philosophy. Perhaps I should, or could, have found a stronger & nobler adjective for the light, to be in greater opposition to the very real crudity of the lump of the earth. And is the internal rhyme in the last line but one effective? I think so. Do let me know what you think of the poem, & soon, if you can.

Love,
DYLAN.

Don't bother too much about other details in it; apart from what I've mentioned, it's the spirit of this poem that matters.

A comparison between this early version which appeared, with two adjectival changes, in Life and Letters Today *(October 1939) and the poem printed in* Deaths and Entrances *and finally in* Collected Poems *shows that all the changes made in its re-writing were movements away from ironical, and towards religious, statement.*

POEM
(To Caitlin)

Unluckily for a death
Waiting with phoenix under a stone
And long fidelity grown grey in her lop-briared
And thigh-describing wreath
Intact among the passionate dead and gone
In the burial holes of enticement
Though the brawl of the kiss has not occurred,
On the wanting mouth,
On the split, exhibiting forehead,
That binds her constant,
Nor the naked, original, lyrical
Agression of love in a bridal broth
Or a continent-sheeted bed with animal rails
And a tucked crust of fossils,

Loving on a sea-banged shelf
My lucky burly body
Holy happy and greedy under the managed storm,
Luckily my sore ghost
In this collapsing day, the dark our pity,
Cut in this mustard moment, soothed of fever
By your kind health that keeps the west wrongs calm,
Fireworks at your breast,
And weeps on the inflammable gulf,

Myself will never
Arch that turkey's neck of a far-gone woman
To sing underground like a married thrush
Or shoo up the light that extinct, sparkling bird to heaven:
The dust-drenched two must wait my wish.

I see the tigron in tears
In the androgynous dark
To escape from the hot, brown caves and ramming columns
Of his half families
That stripe the forests with want, and the duck-
Billed platypus broody in the sexless bush.
There from a red and white clot of women
Juan runs like the waters.
In an imagining of tumbled mantime
Suddenly cold as fish,
I see through briar and stone, the black our business,
That patient love below and almost mistress,
Through masterless ground all loaded events of her flesh,
Great crotch, and giant continence.

Love, my fate got luckily,
May teach me now with no telling
That every drop of water is both kind and cruel,
With articulate eyes
Tell me the money-coloured sun sees poorly,
Teach that the child who sucks on innocence
Is spinning fast and loose on a fiery wheel,
All that we do, cruelly, kindly,
Will kiss in a huddle:
In the teeth of that black-and-white wedding
I chuck my armed happiness.
Though the puffed phoenix stir in the rocks
And lucklessly fair or sycorax the widow wait,
We abide with our pride, the unalterable light,
On this turning lump of mistakes.

Dear Vernon,

I don't find your way of criticizing at all irritating; you know that. It's the most helpful there is for me, and I want it to go on. About many suggestions of yours we'll always, of course, disagree, especially when they seem completely to misunderstand my meaning; but, as nobody else has done—though this is a late and wrong place for a recommendation of your complete intellectual honesty, a thing we needn't talk about—without rancour, affectation, or the felt need to surprise. I think you are liable, in your criticisms of me, to underrate the value—or, rather, the integrity, the wholeness—of what I am saying or trying to make clear that I am saying, and often to suggest alterations or amendments for purely musical motives. For instance, "Caught in a somersault of tumbled mantime" may (and I doubt it) sound more agreeable—we'll leave out any suggestion of it sounding inevitable because it is, however good the implied criticism, a group of words *outside* the poem—to the "prophesying ear" than "In an imagining of tumbled mantime", a line I worked out *for* its sounds & not in spite of them. My criticism of your critical suggestion in this case is that your 'ear' is deaf to the logic of my poem;

> "Caught in a somersault etc etc
> Suddenly cold as fish"

is an ambiguous tangle, very like nonsense. (I know your suggestion was not meant to be the last substitutive word for my first words, but was meant mainly to suggest further things, allway pointers, to me myself; but the suggestion still does, I believe, show the way your criticism often works: towards the aural betterment (ugh) of details, without regard for their significance in a worked-out, if not a premeditated-*in-detail*, whole). This is certainly one critical way, but when it suggests "withered" for "sheeted" in the last line but one of the first stanza, *I* suggest it cuts across the poem and does not come out of it. It is a poet saying "This is what I would have done"; not a critic saying, "This, I think, is what the poet should have done". I suppose, argumentatively, not randomly speaking, that all criticism which is not an analysis of reasons for praise must primarily be suspicion; and that's stimulating. Nothing but the inevitable can be taken for granted, and it always excites me to find you dealing suspiciously with a word, a line, that I had, in a naturally blind or artificially blinkered moment, taken, my-self, with too much trust, trusting too much the fallible creative rush of verse—small or large rushes of verse—that comes, in many cases, between the mechanical preparations for that (in a way) accidental rush. (Wooly writing, I'm afraid; I hope the meaning comes clearly.) With your annoyance at the word "chuck" I agree; and my use of it is sentimental. I have tried "cast", but that is too static a word; I'll find what I really want. And, yes the poem did appear to tire of itself at the end—: (by the way, I resent that 'tire of itself' idea, which arrogantly supposes the self-contained *identity* of the poem even in its forming phases; the poem is not, of course, itself until the poet has left it). The jingle of "abide with our pride" I'm retaining; I wanted the idea of an almost jolly jingle there, a certain carelessness to lead up to the flat, hard, ugly last line of truth, a suggestion of "Well, that's over, O atta boy we live with our joy"; a purposeful intolerance—no, I meant an intolerance on purpose—of the arguments I had been setting against my own instinctive delight in the muddled world. Whether that intolerance, carelessness, etc. is *poetically* effec-tive is another kettle of wishes.

It is very fine news of the masque, and Caitlin and I will be there. We will try to bring Hughes too. Why don't you write to him? You want a big audience, of word-boys as well as theatre boys. Who have you asked? I shall do a review for Life & Letters, but after the show you must let me read the masque. We'll be there for the First Night, I hope.

We want a little poem for Llewelyn.

Love till we see you; and before and after. Can you come &

see Norman Cameron? He'll be down for a weekend soon, I'll let you know when.

Write soon. Here is a new short poem, nothing very much.

DYLAN.

The word I used too much—"sucked"—is here bound, I think, to be.

"Desireless familiar" is a phrase in my "Orchards" & what caused me to write the poem. The best thing is, as you'll perhaps agree, the simple last line of the middle bit.

[Enclosed with this letter:]

TO OTHERS THAN YOU.

Friend by enemy I call you out.

You with a bad coin in your socket,
You my friend there with a winning air
Who palmed the lie on me when you looked
Brassily at my shyest secret,
Enticed with twinkling bits of the eye
Till the sweet tooth of my love bit dry,
Rasped at last, and I stumbled and sucked,
Whom now I conjure to stand as thief
In the memory worked by mirrors,
With unforgettably smiling act,
Quickness of hand in the velvet glove
And my whole heart under your hammer,
Were once such a creature, so gay and frank
A desireless familiar
I never thought to utter or think
While you displaced a truth in the air,

68

That though I loved them for their faults
As much as for their good
My friends were enemies on stilts
With their heads in a cunning cloud.

———

I had hoped that Dylan would be able to see a Masque of mine,
The Influences, *performed by the Swansea Little Theatre.*
Richard and Frances Hughes managed to get to the performance,
but Dylan and Caitlin did not.

[Undated: must be July 1939; envelope dated 4/7/1939]
Sea View, Laugharne.

Dear Vernon,

This is to tell you, with great regret, that we *may* not be able to come to your play. If Hughes can come—he's not sure yet, he may have to go to London—then we'll be able to; if not, not. I thought I'd have some money this week, but bills took it at once & now we couldn't afford to go to Carmarthen even. But *if* Hughes can go, he'll take us & then everything will be all right. I'd hate to have to miss the play, more than I can tell you. Cameron was supposed to have come here last weekend, but cdn't manage it. Instead, Roger Roughton drove John Davenport down in an impossibly luxurious car; they returned yesterday. I hope very very much to be able to see you on Thursday night; and we *will* try. But if we can't, you must get the Theatre to give us a private performance later on.

Love from us both,
DYLAN.

Dylan Thomas's third book, The Map of Love, *had now been published by Dent's. Herbert Read, among others, had acclaimed the poems, and Desmond Hawkens, the former Editor of* Purpose, *had reviewed the book in* The Spectator.

Professor Thomas Taig, of Swansea University, had produced

*my Masque, played by the Swansea Little Theatre which he
founded, in July. He was now planning a further production at
the Mercury Theatre in London, in a programme which would
combine a reading of poems by Welsh writers with two one-act
plays.*

Saturday: [envelope dated 25th August 1939]
Sea View, Laugharne

Dear Vernon,

Sorry not to have written before. I've been busy—over
stories, pot-boiling stories for a book, semi-autobiographical,
to be finished by Christmas—lazy—messing about in the sun
and pub—and worried, by the nearness of this monstrous and
still incredible war. No, my book couldn't have come out in a
viler month; almost as bad as some woman I was told of who
published her first (&, since, her only) novel on the day of the
opening of the General Strike & did not have one single review
or advertisement (no papers were printed for a week); & not
one single copy of the book was sold. I haven't seen Hawkens's
Spectator review yet; hope to get it sent on in a day or two.
I saw the imbecile Western Mail with striking, if podgy,
photograph.

Your Masque I left with my father in Bishopston. Can you
call there for it, or shall I write to him asking him to send it on
to you?

This war, trembling over on the edge of Laugharne, fills me
with such horror & terror & lassitude that I can't easily think
about the London programme. I've selected a good number of
poems—including some by Alan Pryce-Jones which, in their
very worldly & wellbred way, are really beautiful. None by
you. You can either send a ballad or two to Taig, or wait until
we all three meet. Perhaps the last would be the best. I didn't
want to select anything of yours without your approval, and
anyway I haven't much of yours at hand. Taig suggests only
20 minutes for the short poems; I say at least 1/2 hour. But

everything—including all our happiness—depends on Hitler, Poland, & insanity.

I'm afraid I shan't be able to come Swansea way for a while. If there's no war I'll be broadcasting, with Keidrych, from Swansea on the 6th of September, 6.40 to 7. Could we meet you in Swansea afterwards for a drink? I think I'll try to return to Laugharne that same evening.

Laugharne is a little Danzig.

Wish I could see you soon. When can you can you come down?

Caitlin & Llewelyn are well.

Love to you from us,
DYLAN.

Regards to your family.

On the day of the outbreak of war Taig drove me in his car to Laugharne. We heard the news of Chamberlain's announcement on the way. Brown's Hotel in Laugharne was full of villagers and soldiers, among them two military policemen who had come to collect deserters but were now drinking with them. We left them on the friendliest terms late in the evening.

[*No date: September 1st 1939*] *Sea View, Laugharne*
Dear Vernon,

War seems to have begun. But do come on Sunday, if you can. With Taig too. Any time? Will you make it lunch? If so, arrive by one, please. Perhaps you can let us know—phone—in the Saturday evening.

What are you going to do in the war? I can't kill & so, I suppose, will have to join the dangerous RAMC.

Looking forward to you.

Keidrych & Heseltine came down yesterday. Went back this morning.

Love to you & family from us.

DYLAN.

But is there
any reason
against you
coming down here in the weekend?

Thursday: [*envelope dated 29th September 1939*]
Dear Vernon,

We were all ready to come when bills came too, and, to our disgust, we felt we should pay them at once with the money we were intending for our Swansea visit. We did. Caitlin and I were very sorry to miss Dot once again. Just as we're about to come, we have a wire from you saying 'Dot is here', & our plans, quite soon after, are changed. Just as we used to leave the day before she came. All that's unfortunate & accidental, as you might know: we'd love to see you & Dot right now but we have to stay here with a baby and a new kitten called Pussy. I hope a lot we can come to see you soon. Write to me. Poems? I want to have everything (except aeroplanes)

Love, to all,

DYLAN & CAITLIN

The World I Breathe *was published by New Directions; the title was taken from the first line of one of the* Twenty-five Poems:

To-day, this insect, and the world I breathe.

The 'Cough' *story was* 'Extraordinary Little Cough', *later collected in* Portrait Of The Artist As A Young Dog. '*Rough Sea*' *refers to my* 'Ballad Of The Rough Sea'.

The Mercury Theatre show did not materialize, as the theatre was closed through the war emergency.

72

Sea View, Laugharne, Sept. 29. 1939

Dear Vernon,

I haven't written all this month because there's been no
news of any importance—only the War—and I've been busy,
too, with my innocent stories. I've written to a few people,
asking them about the difficulties, you know which ones, but
nothing has come of it, and I intend registering as a conscientious objector as soon as necessary.

I suppose you've heard that Keidrych is to be married in
Llanstephan next Wednesday. I am to be best man. Have you
got a respectable suit you can lend me, or, rather, trust me
with? I'll return it, unegged, straight after the wedding—the
next day, really, I can't undress in the church porch. I shall
hardly ever, if ever, need a respectable suit again & it would be
silly of me to put myself in more debt by getting a new suit for
this one remarkable occasion. You're the only chap about my
size. Two men could go in one of Hughes's suits, though he has
offered me one with tails. (that looks like rails, doesn't it?) I'll
take great care of it if you would lend one? Caitlin, who has a
very odd creation to wear, with different coloured sleeves &
frills,—she had it made some time ago, by mistake—promises
her personal supervision of the suit. And its neatly-packed,
punctual return.

My Collected Works—or, really, 40 poems & 12 stories—
are to be published in America in December with the pathetic
title of 'The World I Breathe'. I objected to the title, but was
told it would sell like cakes there. It's a title, I believe, based
on Gone With The Wind. Did you read my "Cough" story
in Life & Letters? The others in my coming book are all like
that, though not exactly. Your *Rough Sea* looked splendid. I
read it aloud again & woke the baby.

Have you seen Taig recently? Is there a chance of the show
coming off this year?

Caitlin (and I) wants to tell Dot that she is very something
or other not to come down and visit us & stay with us for as
long as she can bear it. September is by far the loveliest

month here. Make her come, please. And when are you coming.
I haven't seen you for more than a day & a bit for more than a
year or more.

Do see if you can lend me a suit. All care and gratitude too.
I've only got a pair of baggy trousers & a damp leather coat.

Love to you,

DYLAN.

Regards to your family.

Sunday: [*envelope dated 8th October 1939*]

Sea View, Laugharne, Carmarthenshire

Dear Vernon,

First: many, many thanks for the supersmart suit in which
no moth-holes could be seen and which suited me, apart from
a hesitation at the waist, very well indeed. I looked neat, clean,
and quite prosperous. It's grand of you to let me keep it: I am
now ready for all sartorial occasions, so long as at some of them
I can appear in jersey & corduroys & at others in a smart brown
suit, slightly open in the middle, with its pockets full of rice.

Perhaps you've been seeing Keidrych; when he left us, he
didn't know whether they were going to Swansea or Cardiff;
but I imagine Swansea won. If you have seen him, you know
all about the wedding; if not, I can tell you that it was dis-
tinguished mostly by the beauty of the female attendants, the
brown suit of the best man, [etc.]

We're hoping to come to Bishopston for a few days very
soon; mostly to have a bath, as there's no water in Laugharne
& I smell like an old beaver. I'll try hard to get there: it'll be
good to see you again & to talk & listen.

Thank you again, &

our love & mine,

DYLAN

On my way back from a holiday abroad I had stayed in Laugharne and recited to Dylan the great Yeats poems which I had seen printed in the London Mercury *a few months after his death: 'Lapis Lazuli', 'The Statues', 'Long-Legged Fly' and 'News For The Delphic Oracle'. That was in the summer, and the poems made an unforgettable impression on him.*

Sea View, Laugharne, Carmarthenshire, Monday [Nov? 1939]
Dear Vernon:
I'm going to talk to the English Club at Cambridge on December 7. Not talk, but read poems. I want to read one of yours—what do you suggest?—and some of the very last Yeats, some of those lovely poems you said down here a few months ago when we were walking down a hill. Could you copy a few of those Yeats out for me—& also one or two recommended poems of your own. I'm going to read some Hardy, one Ransome [sic], one Hart Crane, one Auden, one Spender, some Henry Miller, a bit of Nightwood, one or two of my own, one decorative Wallace Steevens [sic]. Any suggestions? Would you like to copy out a few odd poems, anybody's? But anyway do send the Yeats, & yours.
News in another letter.

Love,

DYLAN.

The next letter refers to my poem 'Portrait Of a Friend', based on Dylan's own photograph, which had been sent to me earlier in the year. The poem, afterwards included in my first book, had just come out in Life and Letters.

Sea View, Laugharne, Carmarthenshire, Nov. 10 1939
[pencil]
Dear Vernon,
Thank you a great lot for the present—for the poem and the money. I liked both immensely. The poem, I think, is altogether successful. And thank you for the great Yeats poems;

I'll read them all, of course. The poem of yours that you sent with them is a serious failure, I think—I mean it is a serious poem which fails. *The Windows*, I can't say much about it here and now, but I'll be coming to Swansea at the very beginning of December, all being well & I'd like very much to go through it with you then. The fifth verse particularly struck me as ugly & over-worked. The whole poem, to me, creaks & blunders, although some isolated bits I like & remember. It's altogether too ponderous & stuffy for me; it *is* a camphored elegy—mothballs. But don't mind my rudeness, I'll tell you my real & detailed objections to the poem later. They might amuse you anyway. This is a dirty note.—I can't find a pen. Better one coming *before* we meet, & that should be on the 1st of December.

Thank you again for the terribly kind postal order, the Yeats, The Windows (an admiring boo from me) & Life & Letters which I thought had only your poem to redeem it this month; but what a grand redemption.

Very much love
from
DYLAN.

Love from the family to yours.

Sea View, Laugharne, 30 Nov. 1939

Dear Vernon,

Would you mind forwarding this letter to Taig? I've been asked to do a one-act play here for something or other, & can't think of a play—I want Taig's advice. Lost his address.

We'll be seeing you v. soon now, I hope.

Love,
DYLAN.

The Postscript of the next letter refers to Dylan's Portrait Of The Artist *story, 'The Fight', which I had read in* Life and Letters.

Sea View, Laugharne, Carmarthenshire, December 13 1939
Dear Vernon,

What do I want for Christmas? Oh, that's nice. I want a war-escaper—a sort of ladder, I think, attached to a balloon,— or a portable ivory tower or a new plush womb to escape back into. Or a lotion for invisibility. I don't want a cathedral—you said I couldn't have one—so can I have a dear book? If you like best giving toys or games, could I perhaps have the New Yorker Annual (published by Hamish Hamilton at, I believe, ten & six) which is all funny drawings, half a game, half a book? I should like that very much indeed.

As for Llewelyn, a poem in his stocking is more than he deserves—unless you think, as I think, that everybody deserves everything or nothing. And if you want to add a croaking duck or floating frog, that'll be lovely, the boy is no zoologist and likes, better than anything else in the world, sucking. I can't pretend that he will admire the poem, even if it's grand which I hope and wish, but we will. We send our love, and will be coming up next Thursday. My sister is going to drive us. Of course we're looking forward to seeing you: a silly way of saying we'd fly up if we could, before that. But there will be Christmas Eve for us, and we'll smoke your ridiculous cigarettes and buy bathfuls of cointreau, bitter, biddy, or ink. For you this Christmas a record: which?

The land, the air, Elizabeth, Trouts or Surprises?
Thank you for the New Yorker Annual.

DYLAN.

I'm so glad you liked the fresh, Dan story. I've finished the book now and have nothing to do but wait for Swansea, marble-town, city of laughter, little Dublin, home of at least 2 great men.

The next letters all come from Ringwood. The poem referred to in the second part of the following one is 'Once Below A Time', which was omitted from Deaths And Entrances *but published in* Collected Poems. *The punning 'Wales' was not afterwards changed.*

The new poem, unfinished when this letter was written but sent to me soon after, was 'There Was A Saviour'.

When Dylan had read me some of the stories of Portrait Of The Artist As A Young Dog *I had suggested that he should scrap the title and name the book after one of the stories.*

[Undated: envelope dated 30 January 1940]
Blashford, Ringwood, Hants.

Dear Vernon,

Thank you for typing the poem. And for wanting to get Llewelyn something for his birthday. That's tomorrow. I wish I could have written to you, asking, from him, what he wanted before this, but we've been staying with Joey the ravisher. You will be interested to know that she is appearing in a pantomime—Cecil Beaton's snob show for the troops—dressed as a scarlet & gold satin admiral. She'd knock you cold. Caitlin says that Llewelyn needs most of all: undervests and/or nappies. Is that too dull? she asks. Perhaps it would be easier for her to get them in Ringwood—unless you feel strong enough to ask for them in the Kiddies' Department, and anyway it's difficult to tell you what size he is. So, if, again, you don't think underwear a very happy present for a one year old boy, perhaps you'd like to send a little bit of What Matters on to Caitlin (*marginal note:* I'm not sure if those negatives make sense) & she'll buy the things & you shall see Llewelyn in them—if you've got eyes that penetrate outer wrappings, or even if Caitlin shows you—when we return to Bishopston in about 10 days time. Llewelyn says Ta to you—*and* ba, da, ma.

I agreed with your criticism of the 'lubber crust of Wales' but have, so far, done nothing about altering it. Gaels is good, but that too sounds to me facietious [sic]. Actually, although I thought the pun out quite coldly, I wanted to make the lubber line a serious one, and I'm glad that you like it apart from its joke. I'll tell you, later, what I do about it: I shall probably use Gaels, anyway. Now I'm working on a new poem, a poem which is giving me more pleasure than I've got out of any work for months, or even years. Yes, the Lawrence calling-up-of-memory in the kangaroo lines was intentional, but if in any way it seems feeble, perhaps a little tame, in such a poem (strenuously resisting conventional associations) then, of course, I must change it. I'll let you know when I come back to the poem. As it is, changing only the word 'Wales' I might print the poem in L & Letters just as it is, alterable bits & all; & then work on it later. I see nothing silly in that. I didn't like much "I do not regret the bugle I wore" but its omission makes the end too vague. I'll either retain the line or alter it—alter it, that is, in a worked-on version later. I'll send you the new poem v. soon. I've just finished my Portrait. . . . Young Dog proofs. Out in March. I've kept the flippant title for—as the publishers advised—moneymaking reasons.

I'll be writing when the poem's finished. Love, & thanks for poem, criticism, & godfatherliness.

D.

The artist Mervyn Levy, a Swansea friend of Dylan's, was a very good mimic of Groucho Marx. Dylan himself resembled Harpo (and the boy who delivered papers at his Swansea house used to call him Harpo) so they frequently played the two parts together.

The poem discussed in the second paragraph of the next letter is again 'Once Below A Time'.

The short poems I wrote for my godson, 'Poems for Llewelyn', appeared in Life and Letters *soon after this.*

My sister Dot is often mentioned in the letters. Again and again she happened to arrive home just when Dylan had gone, or else he in coming would miss her by a day.

Dear Vernon,

Thank you—Caitlin is writing separately—for the present for Llewelyn, who is an intolerable dandy and shames his stained and smoky father. He also had a suit from grandparents, and a musical box, and the most menacing, lunatic doll, half Mervyn Levy, half Harpo Marx, that I have ever seen—with a twitching head and revolving ears—and some napkins and barley sugar and a cake (with one candle) which his cousin ate.

For 'I do not regret', in my much discussed poem, I have put 'Never never oh never to regret the bugle I wore' (all one line), so that the repetition, the pacific repetition, of 'I would lie down, lie down, lie down and live' is loudly and swingingly balanced. When you see the poem again, I think you'll like the alteration.

I'm glad Herring is going to print some Llewelyn poems. Little the little one knows. Our family is very proud of the poems.

The dim snaps were liked a lot.

Is Dot still with you? We will miss her easily this time.

Our love to her & you, and all.

DYLAN.

P.S.
This all is
shockingly late
because Caitlin
thought I'd
posted it &
I thought she
had. Also
I've been in
bed for 3
days—just
up now—with

a huge cough &
cold.
Write soon, & I
will too.

*The lyrical poem referred to at the beginning of the next letter
is 'There Was A Saviour', Line 3 of the last verse of this poem
was originally written as:*

Deaths of the only ones, our never found.

*The satirical poem about war-time London is 'The Country-
man's Return'.*
*The Ballad he asks me to send is 'The Ballad Of The Mari
Lwyd' which I had just finished. I had quoted a part of it to him
at Laugharne, but he did not see it until he stayed with me later,
when I read him the whole poem.*
*The Postscript above the letter concerns Virgil's Fourth
Eclogue, translated by James Laughlin, published as a Christmas
card for James Laughlin by his firm, New Directions. This translation is included in the American* Little Treasury of World
Poetry *edited by Hubert Creekmore and published by Scribner's.*

Blashford, Ringwood

P.S. The Virgil ode I said I was
enclosing won't fit in the
envelope. Sorry. I'll buy
a big envelope this week.

March 6 1940

Dear Vernon,
I'm so glad you liked my lyrical poem, that you thought it
was one of my best. I'll think of 'stupid kindred', which is
right, of course, in meaning and which prevents any ambiguity,
but kindred seems a little pompous a word: it hasn't the literal
simplicity of hindering man. No, I can't see 'seep' with dust,

F 81

& unless a better word can be made will remain true to 'fly'. But about line 3 of the last verse, you're right as can be, and somehow I must make 'death' the second word. I'll let you know what I can work out. I like the word 'blacked', by the way, in spite of its, in the context, jarring dissonance with 'locked'. I had, quite apart (that is absurd, I mean secondarily to) from the poem, the blackout in mind, another little hindrance on the scene, & the word seemed, to me, to come rightly. But I'll think about it. Your criticism's always terribly suggestive, & in that particular 'death line' you showed quite clearly to me the one big misbalance in the poem. Ta. I'm writing an awkward, satirical poem about war-time London now: a kind of elaborate, rough, angry joke which Keidrych would like a lot. You shall see it, of course; you might like it too, with all the proper reservations: I had to have a change after my austere poem in Milton measure.

And now I want very much to see the long-waited-for Ballad. Would it be too much work for you to copy me a copy? I thought I'd be back in Wales early this month, but I may have to go up to London to see about a possible, but very improbable, job that would keep me from pleading or soldiering. To do with films: I shan't get it. But if I do have to go up to town, it means I shan't be home for a bit of time & I must see the Ballad before that. Do, please. I'm glad you're happy from it. It must be very good.

Has Life & Letters come out yet? I haven't been sent my copy. Thank you for wanting to give Llewelyn the quid from the Llewelyn poems. But Caitlin says he's got plenty of clothes now; and if you'd like to send me the quid, or 14/- of it, you'd save us losing our bed. The bed on which you have slept in Laugharne is being bought on hire-purchase from a shop in Swansea at 7 bob a month, and we owe them 2 months on it—no 3 including this, I forgot—and they're going to do something cruel with solicitors unless we pay immediately. And I'm without a penny and hopelessly in debt, here as well as in Laugharne. I think it would be very nice for Llewelyn's poems to save our bed. (Our cardboard bed, do you remember it?) Llewelyn's bronchitis is better, and today he is out in the sun. I'll send you my awkward poem in a day or two. But let me have the ballad. I'll recite it to the collected household. Caitlin's mother is waiting, too, to read the poems to her grandchild: I have only the prologue with me here. I'm enclosing Laughlin's Christmas card.

Love to you from Caitlin & me,
& to your family.

Since this—I lost the post—I've been reading the (my) poem very carefully, and have made these slight but, I think important (relatively) alterations: "*And laid your cheek against a cloud-formed shell*". This harder word, 'formed', balances the line, avoids the too-pretty internal rhyme of 'laid' & 'made', & stops the too easy flow, or thin conceited stream. |

To avoid ambiguity, & also the use of the word 'kindred' I've turned 'his' in line 6 of verse 2 into 'that'.

In the last verse, the 3rd line now is: "Brave deaths of only ones, but never found", which I believe to be right. Do look at it carefully. For 'fly' in the last line but 2 of last verse I have now 'ride'. I'm sure of that: it's mysteriously militant, which is what I wanted.

The satirical poem of the third paragraph of the next letter is ' The Countryman's Return', sent a week or so later. The Ballad he asks for is again my ' Ballad Of The Mari Lwyd' which at that moment, after the long period of composition, seemed to me too recently finished to send away. When he did see it he recommended one alteration, that the first line of the Prologue should not be repeated at the end of the Prologue. I took his advice and deleted the repetition.

Blashford, Ringwood [*address not in D's handwriting*]

[*No date; March 1940*]

Dear Vernon,

Thank you so much for the bedsaver; it has. Lovely of you, and one day I will buy you a bank all for yourself.

I've no news. We're just hanging on here until I hear, or don't, from London where I *may* be offered a job, though it's improbable.

I've not finished my satirical poem yet, & have, for the want of satirical feeling, left it for a time to begin an ambitious new poem. Sorry you can't send the Ballad, I must see it soon.

Thank you—I nearly forgot—for Life & Letters; mine came today. The Llewelyn poems were appreciated by everyone; I liked, myself, the Dalai Lama poem particularly. Apart from you & me, I didn't like much in the number, & thought Glyn Jones's story affected & imitative. Peter Helling's got something. 'Got something', my God. Am I trying to be a Little Master.

Thank you again, & love from the both of us. News, I hope, soon; & we're longing to return. South England is a flat green plate covered with soldiers.

DYLAN.

The next letter is entirely concerned with ' The Countryman's Return', and its variants. The text printed here is copied from the manuscript. The cinematographic background recalls the same device in the earlier poem ' Then Was My Neophyte':

> He films my vanity.
> Shot in the wind by tilted arcs,
> Over the water come
> Children from homes and children's parks
> Who speak on a finger and thumb
> And the masked, headless boy.

His reels and mystery
The winder of the clockwise scene
Wound like a ball of lakes
Then threw on that tide-hoisted screen
Love's image till my heartbone breaks
By a dramatic sea.

'The Countryman's Return' was printed in The Cambridge Front *(Summer, 1940), the missing word of line 75 being 'porches'.*

Blashford, Ringwood, March 19. 1940

Dear Vernon,

Here's my 100 line satirical poem. I'm sure you won't like it. Or am I sure? It isn't, by a long something, your favourite kind, but you like all kinds and may appreciate—(not the word) —this half comic attack on myself. I've got very little to say about it myself: you'll see the heavy hand with which I make fun of this middle-class, beardless Walt who props humanity, in his dirty, weeping, expansive moments, against corners & counters & tries to slip, in grand delusions of all embracing humanitarianism, everyone into himself. The first 'Cut' in the last verse is, of course, cinema. And a loud Stop. The heaviest satire against myself (or the figure I have made myself into) is in the 7th to the 13th line of the last verse. Then, in the very last part, by a change of rhythm I try to show the inevitability of my unrepentance of the charges that the rollicking attack has made. The whole thing's bristling with intentional awkwardnesses, grotesque jokes, vulgarities of phrasing; but I know it *is* a whole thing, & that's something. Tell me. I shan't alter much of it anyway: it's not the sort of poem to try to polish; in fact, I've tried to avoid most slicknesses, which might have come so easily. This proud talk is only because I've just finished.

85

I may be back on Thursday, unless I'm called to town. I'll
let you know.

My love,
Ever,

DYLAN

Could you type all this? I've no-one else to help me in *any*
way about poems.

[*On reverse of letter:*]
Cut. Cut the crushed streets, leaving
A hole full of errands and shades;
Plug the paper-blowing tubes;
Emasculate the seedy clocks;
Rub off the scrawl of prints on
Body and air and building;
Branch and leaf the birdless roofs;
Faces of melting visions,
Magdalene prostitution,
Glamour of the bloodily bowed,
Exaltation of the blind,
That sin-embracing dripper of fun
Sweep away like a cream cloud;
Bury all rubbish and love signs
Of my week in the dirtbox
In this anachronistic scene   Sawing
Where I sit in laundered linen
In a hutch in cow-patched fields,
Flat green plates of lavabread

Where sitting in laundered linen
In a hutch in cowpatched fields
I hear the familiar birds
Sawing through my sober veins,
I Delight, I suppose, in
The countryman's stumbling back
And count on pretty leaves,

up
Birds' legs, bull's blood
~~All~~ rusticating minutes,
The wasteful hushes among trees.

                              with sparrows on it

Where sitting in laundered linen
In a hutch in cowpatched glen
~~I suppose I now delight in~~
Now I delight, I suppose, in
The countryman's stumbling back
And count by birds' ~~legs~~ eggs & leaves
~~All~~ The rusticating minutes,
The wasteful hushes among trees.

————————————————————

————————————————————

Cut. Cut the green fields, leaving
The streets and their destinities.

And o to cut the green field, leaving
One street with ~~hunger~~ in it
    ~~dark~~   ~~people~~
    ~~rich~~   ~~desire~~

[*On separate sheet:*]

THE COUNTRYMAN'S RETURN

Embracing low-falutin
London (said the odd man in
A country pot, his hutch in
The fields, by a motherlike henrun)
With my fishtail hands and gently
Manuring popeye or
Swelling in flea-specked linen
The rankest of the city
I spent my unwasteable
Time among walking pintables

87

With sprung and padded shoulders,
Tomorrow's drunk club majors
Growing their wounds already,
The last war's professional
Unclaimed dead, girls from good homes
Studying the testicle
In communal crab flats
With the Sunflowers laid on,
Old paint-stained tumblers riding
On stools to a one man show down,
Gasketted and sirensuited
Bored and viciously waiting
Nightingales of the casualty stations
In the afternoon wasters
White feathering the living.

London's arches are falling
In, in Pedro's or Wendy's
With a silverfox farmer
Trying his hand at failing
Again, a collected poet
And some dismantled women,
Razor man and belly king,
I propped humanity's weight
Against the fruit machine,
Opened my breast and into
The spongebag let them all melt.
Zip once more for a traveller
With his goods under his eyes,
Another with hers under her belt,
The black man bleached to his tide
Mark, trumpet lipped and blackhead
Eyed, while the tears drag on the tail,
The weighing-scales, of my hand.
Then into blind streets I swam
Alone with my bouncing bag,

Too full to bow to the dim
Moon with a relation's face
Or lift my hat to unseen
Brothers dodging through the fog
The affectionate pickpocket
And childish, snivelling queen.

Beggars, robbers, inveiglers,
Voices from manholes and drains,
Maternal short time pieces,
Octopuses in doorways,
Dark inviters to keyholes
And evenings with great danes,
Bedsitting girls on the beat
With nothing for the metre,
Others whose single beds hold two
Only to make two ends meet,
All the hypnotised city's
Insidious procession
Hawking for money and pity
Among the hardly possessed.
And I in the wanting sway
Caught among never enough
Conjured me to resemble
A singing Walt from the mower
And jerrystone trim villas
Of the upper of the lower half,
Beardlessly wagging in Dean Street,
Blessing and counting the bustling
Twolegged handbagged sparrows,
Flogging into the   [porches]
My cavernous, featherbed self.

Cut. Cut the crushed streets, leaving
A hole of errands and shades;
Plug the paper-blowing tubes;

Emasculate the seedy clocks;
Rub off the scrawl of prints on
Body and air and building;
Branch and leaf the birdless roofs;
Faces of melting visions,
Magdalene prostitution,
Glamour of the bloodily bowed,
Exaltation of the blind,
That sin-embracing dripper of fun
Sweep away like a cream cloud;
Bury all rubbish and love signs
Of my week in the dirtbox
In this anachronistic scene
Where sitting in clean linen
In a hutch in a cowpatched glen
Now I delight, I suppose, in
The countryman's return
And count by birds' eggs and leaves
The rusticating minutes,
The wasteful hushes among trees.
And O to cut the green field, leaving
One rich street with hunger in it.

Laugharne, Tuesday [*1940*]

Dear Vernon,

TA for the great pound. I heard it singing in in the envelope.

Be an R.A.F. officer. You're too senile to fly, and there's obviously more time to write poems when you're an officer than when you're creeping round corners slow as snails on your motorised scooter.

Ring up Laugharne 3 and say that you'll come *this* weekend. We want you to very much.

TA again, & be sure to come down, please.

Love
DYLAN.

The next letter was entirely devoted to a single poem, and with it arrived the version following of 'Unluckily For A Death', considerably altered subsequently, though the title was kept. I told him that I thought the last line of this version too much a silhouette line, too slight a line to end the poem. A comparison with the final version in Collected Poems *will show how deeply the revision of the whole last stanza gained in power.*

The Worm, in the middle of the first paragraph of the letter, refers to Worm's Head at the end of the Gower peninsula, jutting out to sea from the six-mile-long Rhossili beach. We had almost been cut off by the tide which comes in very quickly between the rocky coast and the beginning of Worm's Head; we had just reached the land by wading knee-deep. Dylan used to train for long-distance running on Rhossili sands, the setting of his story, 'Extraordinary Little Cough'. He had once been cut off on the Worm; it was before I knew him. He said how cold it had been, and how he had kept warm by running and clapping his hands during his six hours' wait for the sea.

[*Undated: envelope dated 5th June 1940*], Seaview.
Dear Vernon,

The first word since the death of our date in No. 10. when pimples would have put us in our places—though I think Caitlin would have frightened them, not frightened them away, perhaps, but certainly made each blush. What a lot of pities we never could arrange longer and noisier evenings: noisy with our own poems, and even with poor Yeats's or done Pound's. ("Well, what do you think of Paradise Lost?" "It was the title got me.") But we had our moments, I heard Baille's Strand and two, at least, fine ones of your own, we heard Figaro and "I am" very very high up in the Empire roof, Beethoven accompanied our croquet, you nearly caught us napping on the Worm—and what would a stranger, hearing suddenly, make of that?—and, of course, we carefully missed Dot. Is she still in Pennard? Give her our love and tell her that God must consider us allergic: we don't. Can you come down

91

here soon? You & Dot? You? We've distempered the rooms & made a cosy home: come and sit down, talking, on our deceptive chairs, and lie in the stormy bed of which Llewelyn now, most indirectly, owns half a leg—it was the proceeds of a poem to him, do you remember, that saved it.

Here's a poem. I showed you the beginning, or *a* beginning, months—is it?—ago in Laugharne. Tell me straight away. I consider, at the just-finished, illusionary glowing moment, it's good. I've never worked harder on anything, maybe too hard: I made such a difficult shape, too. Points: 1. I want a title for it. Can you suggest? Modern Love? Wd that be affected? I've often wanted to use other people's titles, & once began my Ode On The Intimations Of Immortality. It is a poem about modern love. For some reason, I wrote a note under the poem in my copybook:

All over the world love is being betrayed as always, and a million years have not calmed the uncalculated ferocity of each betrayal or the terrible loneliness afterwards. Man is denying his partner man or woman and whores with the whole night, begetting a monstrous brood; one day the brood will not die when the day comes but will hang on to the breast and the parts and squeeze his partner out of bed. Or, as a title, One Married Pair. It's a poem of wide implications, if not of deep meanings, and I want a matter-of-fact, particular title.

2. "Helled and heavened shell". Is this too clumsy? I like it, but it may be. 3. The longest line in the last verse: is this too—prosy? I wanted a very direct statement, but perhaps this straggles.

Write soon & tell me about yourself your poems & this.

Love,
DYLAN

Will you type the —— ? It's not so easy to type either. Hope you can see the arrangement of the length of lines.

I.

Into her lying down head
His enemies entered bed,
Under the encumbered eyelid,
Through the rippled drum of the hair-buried ear;
And Noah's rekindled now unkind dove
Flew man-bearing there.
Last night in a raping wave
Whales quaked loose from the green grave
In fountains of origin gave up their love,
Along her innocence glided
Juan aflame and savagely young King Lear,
Queen Catherine howling bare
And Samson drowned in his hair,
The colossal intimacies of silent
Once seen strangers or shades on a stair;
There the dark blade and wanton sighing her down
To a haycock couch and the scythes of his arms
Rode and whistled a hundred times
Before the crowing morning climbed;
Enamoured Tahiti and shining Hollywood, Circe's swinish,
coiling island,
Made her limbs blind by luminous charms,
Sleep to a newborn sleep in a swaddling loin-leaf stroked
and sang
And his runaway beloved childlike laid in the acorned
sand.

II.

There where a numberless tongue
Wound their room with a male moan,
His faith around her flew undone
And darkness hung the walls with baskets of snakes,
A furnace-nostrilled column-membered
Super-or-near man

Resembling to their dulled sense
The thief of adolescence,
Early imaginary half remembered
Oceanic lover alone
Jealousy cannot forget for all her sakes,
Made her bad bed in her good
Night, and enjoyed as he would.
Crying, white gowned, from the middle moonlit stages
Out to the tiered and hearing tide,
Close and far she announced the theft of the heart
In the taken body at many ages,
Trespasser and broken bride
Celebrating at his side
All blood-signed assailings and vanished marriages in which
he had no pretty part
Nor could share, for his pride, to the least
Mutter and foul wingbeat of the solemnizing nightpriest
Her holy unholy hours with the always anonymous
beast.

III.

Two sand grains together in bed,
Head to heaven-circling head,
Singly lie with the whole wide shore
The covering sea their nightfall with no names;
And out of every helled and heavened shell
One voice in chains declaims
The female, deadly, and male
Libidinous betrayal,
Golden dissolving under the water veil.
A she bird sleeping brittle by
Her lover's wings that fold tomorrow's flight,
Within her nested treefork
Sings to the treading hawk,
Carrion, paradise, chirrup my bright yolk.

From the madhouses and menageries
Of jealous night uncage the grain and bird:
The love of women and men
Scrapes and sings denied in them,
The filth and secret of death is sweeter with the sun than these
inconstancies,
A loveless man mourns in the sole night.
Betrayed will his love betrayed find an eye or a hair to
hate?
Will his lovely hands let run the daughters and sons of the
blood?
Will he rest his pulse in the built breast of impossible,
great God?
Over the world uncoupling the moon rises up to no good.

*Dylan had now moved to Marshfield, near Chippenham, where
he was living in John Davenport's house with a number of writers,
artists and musicians who had been offered hospitality there.*

*It was through being a professional writer, and not an amateur
as Dylan describes him, that John Davenport was able to offer
this hospitality.*

*I had applied for a Field Security Police job in the Army, but
this involved looking after a motor-cycle and understanding its
engine which I knew I could not do. On Pendine sands, not long
before, we had both been allowed to try to drive a friend's car.
I had no understanding of the controls, and Dylan's maximum
acceleration was ten miles an hour before the car came to rest in
soft sand. Both potential drivers, we blamed the conditions; but,
so far as I know, neither of us ever drove again.*

at The Malting House, Marshfield, nr. Chippenham, Wilts.
8 August, I think [1940]
Dear Vernon,
It shows what a terribly long time we haven't written each

95

other: I've been here for nearly 2 months, and you still think I'm in Laugharne. So I can't come this weekend, however much I want to, and I do want to very much. What a sensational postcard you sent me, & only comfortable, wild Pwll Du on the front. Dot going to Japan & you joining the army; dear God. Have you joined, or are you conscripted? Do tell me everything about it. And why a motorcycle driver? I know what your motor-driving's like from Pendine sands. I'm not going to say *you're* barmy, but the chaps who engaged you to drive on the public roads must be very strange little men with curling beards & tall white hats. But I want to know all about the decision & mystery. Please write soon.

I'm staying here in John Davenport's house. He's an amateur writer & musician, extremely able, weighing nineteen stone. It's a big house, full of books & pianos & records. There are lots of other people staying here too: Lennox Berkeley, Arnold Cooke (who remembers you very well at Repton. Do you remember him?) who are both professional composers, Antonia White, and William Glock. Aren't they nice names? Davenport & I are writing a fantastic thriller together, so I haven't done a poem for a long time although there are 2 I want to write badly: both nightmares, I'm afraid. Oh Europe etcetera please do be bettera.

The other Llewelyn poems are in Life & Letters, are they? I'll get a copy. I want to see them a lot. Llewelyn is with Caitlin's mother at the moment, but we'll have to have him back soon because we both miss him, especially Caitlin.

I don't know what my own plans are. I want a job very badly, because I haven't a penny: quite as a matter of fact, not a penny. If you ever have 5 shillings you hate, I shan't. I've applied for a BBC job, but I think my lack of university will spoil it. It wd be a very well paid job, but boring: making preces (I mean summaries) of the world's news for Empire bulletins.

Caitlin & I go bicycling nearly every day. I love it. I wish

you could come here, I wish I cd see you. Do write straightaway & tell me the whole stories.

I'll write a long letter by return.

Love from C & me,

DYLAN

Remember me to your pa & ma, please

*Pwlldu, which is the Welsh for 'black pool', is a bay at the
bottom of Bishopston Valley, three miles east of Pennard. We
would often go there.*

*The detective story mentioned in the third paragraph of the
next letter from Marshfield was called 'Death of the King's
Canary'; the collaboration was with John Davenport. Dylan read
me most of it, including all the parodies; and he did, I think, read
it on one of his visits to Cambridge. The theme was the death of a
poet laureate and the difficulty of finding his successor. All the
sober candidates refused, and it was left to a drink-loving anarchist
to accept. The butt of Malmsey wine persuaded him. He invited
all the leading literary figures of the day to a banquet of celebra-
tion. Parodies of their works were read at the banquet which became an increasingly embarrassing mixture of squalor, courtesy
and confusion. The guests, all of whom represented contemporary
writers affectionately caricatured, behaved according to their
dignity or lack of it. I describe the book from memory only,
thinking it lost, and that only one parody, 'Homage to William
Empson', which Dylan himself wrote and printed in* Horizon,
*survives. But now a note has come from John Davenport saying
that the manuscript, lost for nearly seventeen years, has turned up
in a deed-box at Marshfield.*

*Dylan's close friend Alfred Janes, the painter, with whom he
had lived in London when he first went there (Mervyn Levy was
the third sharer of their flat), had somehow acquired a reputation
for never writing letters. Nobody had seen a letter from him when*

we used to meet regularly in Swansea. The words 'Life and letter' refer back to a letter from Dylan which I have lost, describing how someone had written to Alfred Janes, 'and', the letter went on, 'actually heard from that umbrella. So now I have decided to abandon the book I was going to write and devote myself to the life and letter of Alfred Janes.'

Malting House, Marshfield, nr. Chippenham, Wilts.

[envelope stamped 1940]

Dear Vernon,

God, yes, how awful it must have looked. But I didn't get the 2 quid. Mad things have been happening to letters: I've lost one before, about 3 weeks ago. I think this house must be marked, & the letters opened. Really. The house, as I told you, is full of musicians, all are young men, not one is in the army, one has a German name, there *was* a German staying here some time ago, and there have also been five lighting offences in about six weeks. Perhaps a lucky censor got your lovely present. I am so sorry, for you & for me. 2 crinklers. And at bank-bombing time too. I thought that your not answering my letter was because you'd been hijacked into the army. I couldn't realize *you* were waiting for an answer from *me*.

I can't imagine Gower bombed. High explosives at Pennard. Flaming onions over Pwlldu. And Union Street ashen. This is all too near. I had to go to London last week to see about a BBC job, & left at the beginning of the big Saturday raid. The Hyde Park guns were booming. Guns on the top of Selfridges. A 'plane brought down in Tottenham Court Road. White-faced taxis still trembling through the streets, though, & buses going, & even people being shaved. Are you frightened these nights? When I wake up out of burning birdman dreams—they were frying aviators one night in a huge frying pan: it sounds whimsical now, it was appalling then—and hear the sound of bombs & gunfire only a little way away, I'm so relieved I could laugh or cry. What *is* so frightening, I think, is

98

the idea of greyclothed, grey-faced, blackarmletted troops marching, one morning, without a sound up a village street. Boots on the cobbles, of course, but no Heil-shouting, grenading, goose-stepping. Just silence. That's what Goebbels has done for me. I get nightmares like invasions, all successful. (Ink gone)

I saw, and of course liked for I'd known nearly all of it before, the Llewelyn poems. Have you any time for writing now? Will you let me see something new? I've collaborated in a detective story and am just about to begin a short story. I do scripts for the BBC, to be translated into, & broadcast to, Brazil. I've got an exciting one to do next, on Columbus. But I haven't settled down to a poem for a long time. I want to, & will soon, but it mustn't be nightmarish. ✕

I just looked again at your last letter, and you said in it that bombs were falling on the cliffs. I hope they missed you. Where is the nearest air-raid shelter? Singleton? You must run very fast. In this house Caitlin & I have our bedroom on the top floor, and so far we haven't got up even when the German machines are over us like starlings. But I think we'll have to, soon. My mother wrote & told me that people are sleeping on the Gower beaches, in barns and hedges. I went to see a smashed aerodrome. Only one person had been killed. He was playing the piano in an entirely empty, entirely dark canteen.

What are our Swansea friends doing? Is Fred still cross-gartering fruit and faces? drilling? objecting? I don't hear from him ever. Life & Letter, of course. My father said he saw him in an airbattle over the town, standing in the middle of the street, his long neck craned.

I don't know at all when we'll be back in the ruins. I'll have to go to London so often, once—& if ever—this job gets really going. I'd love to see you before you undrive your motorcycle. No chance of us meeting in London? We've never done that. That would be lovely.

Write soon. Forgive this unavoidable & rude-appearing

99

delay. Sorry, very sorry, sorrier than I can tell you, about the death of the pounds.

Lower me immediately on the equinoctial list of dislikes.

Love from Caitlin & me.

Remember me to your people. I hope the bombs won't touch the croquet lawn. We must all play next summer.

DYLAN.

Alfred Janes was by this time in the Pioneer Corps. His early still-lifes, based on a meticulous geometry, were executed with an almost fantastic slowness and care.

The story to be called Adventures in the Skin-trade *is the first mention in the letters of the unfinished novel of that title. The poem about invasion is 'Deaths and Entrances'.*

[*No address: postmark from Chippenham*]
[*No date: probably August 1940*]

Dear Vernon,

It was lovely to hear from you. Thank you for the rest of the lost present. It was needed alright,: by others. I'm in debt, & need my job quickly. Perhaps we're both marked. You translate Holderlein [sic] & swear in German to the Home Guards; I have no visible means of support, & have been known to call the war bloody and silly. I hope there's a special censor for our letters: a man who keeps a miserable family on the strength of attempting to decode our innocent messages.

I hope Dot will like Japan. Would she care for me to write to Empson, asking him for addresses of some of his friends? He was there for years, & knows a lot of people. He'd like to. Old Japanese professors. Pale tea & poetry afternoons. I wish we were going there too, I could do with a bit of inscrutability. Europe is hideously obvious and shameless. Am I to rejoice when a 100 men are killed in the air?

Is the Pioneer Corps non-combatant? Was Fred happy about it? Do you know his address? I'd like to write to him, even tho he won't answer. I'll enjoy seeing his war-pictures: the veins of a leaf that blew from a shelled tree; the crisscrosses on the head of a spent bullet. He should do widespread camouflage work, & make Oldham look like the back of a herring.

I can't do much work either. I go for long bicycle rides, thinking: "Here I am on a bicycle in a war." I play whist with musicians, & think about a story I want to call "Adventures in the Skin-trade". I've finished my poem about invasion, but it isn't shapely enough to send you yet.

Remember me to your mother & father.

Don't forget: cover the croquet lawn, bury your poems in a stout box, & don't stare at the sky too much. The wrong wings are up there.

Thank you again. I'll come to Wales soon.

Love,
DYLAN

The prosebook of the second paragraph of the next letter is Adventures in the Skin Trade.

I had at this time suggested the title Gratitude Of A Leper *for my first book of poems which was afterwards called* Ballad Of The Mari Lwyd & Other Poems.

Between the time of the last surviving letter and this one Dylan and Caitlin had had a long stay in Bishopston with his parents. He had lost his ration book, and shortness of money added to his difficulties.

Laugharne Castle, Laugharne, Carmarthenshire
22nd May, 1941

My dear Vernon:

It's been a long pause. And, apart from the loss of your company, a great, sighing relief. I hope we can stay here for a good bit: I have the romantic, dirty summerhouse looking over the marsh to write in, and Caitlin an almost empty, huge room to dance in. Also, we have lots of records now, and we hear, quite often, another word than "ration".

Is Dot home? Our love if she is; or isn't, of course, though it is hard to think with affection of someone in S. Africa. Or to think, perhaps I mean, without envy.

My prosebook's going well, but I dislike it. It's the only really dashed-off piece of work I remember doing. I've done 10,000 words already. It's indecent and trivial, sometimes funny, sometimes mawkish, and always badly written which I do not mind so much.

Any more about your leprous collection? Perhaps the volume should be surgically bound. I do hope it comes out this summer, just before the gas.

When can you come down? There's no room in this house —there are 10 children under 10—but there is in the pub, cheap. Write quickly, and say. You must; we must see you before your new 'Confession of a Dirt-Track Rider'. Because we'll never come back to Bishopston, God's least favourite place. Write this week. Thank you for everything you gave us on our long visit. A little money has arrived for me since your last pound for the road; now that has gone. But anyway we can get so very few cigarettes down here. None now for days. I have taken to biting my nails, but they go down so quickly, and one has only 10.

Well, well, look at the world now.

Love,
DYLAN.

I had sent Dylan my translation of Francis Jammes' 'Prayer to go to Paradise with the Donkeys' which he himself had suggested I should do. It appeared in The Listener *soon afterwards.*

The ballad published in the June number of Horizon *was*

'Ballad of The Long-Legged Bait'. I had watched it grow from fifteen lines to its full length during the stay in Bishopston where he worked at it continuously.

The novel is again Adventures in the Skin Trade. (*In my Foreword to that book I misread the word 'blathers' in this letter as 'blazes'*).

I had lent Dylan a book by Kierkegaard.

Dennis was a young evacuee who lived with my parents for five years.

Laugharne Castle, Laugharne, Carmarthenshire
28 May 1941

My dear V:

Thank you for the letter with Jammes in it. And the round silver trash. Filthy, damned stuff, the halfcrown was the only lovely money I'd seen for a week and more. And it's still all I've seen. This is getting ridiculous. The joke has gone too far. It isn't fair to be penniless *every* morning. Every morning but one, okay; but no, *every* morning.

If you do have a tiny bit to spare, whether it clinks or tinkles, let alone rustles, *do* send it, Vernon. This is absurd. Anything, bled boy, leper, from a penny to a pound. My head's been whirling with wondering how to get twopence, fairly or foully, to put on this nearly a letter. If I fail, it must go naked. Here we are, safe and quiet, and should be happy as cabbages, but it's hard—for me—without a single hour's, half-hour's, minute's, going out in the long, social evening. So if you can don't forget, oh quickly quickly don't forget. I get in such a nagged, impotent, messy state when I'm like this; sit and snap and worry all day; can't be lazy, can't work hard, just sit by myself saying "—— it" in a flat voice. I *do* like that wonderful independence of being able to walk across the road *any* time and buy an envelope or some Vim. Don't forget, like lightning, yours ever,

DYLAN.

My dear V:

I liked the translation enormously much. What a poem! Of course, 'behoves' is right. I read it aloud, slowly, to Caitlin. The music is beautiful. Two possible exceptions: 'poverty' and 'limpidity' so close together; and 'infatuated flies'. Especially the alliteration seems uncertain to me. I'm going to read it again in a minute. Get on with your slow giant Sleeper, I loved the bulls I saw for a moment on the typewriter. And the opening, old lines. You must—can you?—finish it this month, because of the advent of mechanical death. (What a lot of trouble it would have saved if We had sunk the Hood and They the Bismarck). I'm glad you wrote, telling the officials you can only just turn on a bathroom tap. Be a censor: pry and erase. Don't be a cyclist or a parachutist or a mine-tester or the first man on the *very* edge of Dover cliffs.

No, I couldn't do that Ackerley article. I'm not going to talk about poetry now that I have had to, temporarily, stop trying to write it. Besides, he would not print one's truth, because it *would* blast the B.B.C. and every other government institution.

My ballad will be in the June number of Horizon. They haven't printed it nicely: it's in double columns. They wanted more space for an article called 'Whither Solidarity?' or 'An Analysis of Prokosch's Rhythm In His Middle Period'.

My novel blathers on. It's a mixture of Oliver Twist, Little Dorrit, Kafka, Beachcomber, and good old 3-adjectives-a-penny belly-churning Thomas, the Rimbaud of Cwmdonkin Drive.

I was terribly sorry you didn't come down last week-end. It would have been really good. Come down *as soon as* you can. Bring Dot if she's about & will come. Give her our love. I'm afraid I won't be able to meet you in London, or to meet you anywhere further away than walking distance from here. I wish we could meet in the bombs there. But visit us, please.

See if you can squeeze another drop from your borrowed-to-death body. I'm not going to tell you how grateful I am and have always been; or how vile I feel when I ask you again.

Really vile. Weazels take off their hats as I stink by. No, I am sorry. I have no right. I hope I am spoiling nothing. It is just that I am useless, & have nowhere to turn.

I have told Caitlin about Kierkegaard, & he will be sent on, with thanks for him, & love, when we are bloated enough with pennies to be able to bluster into the p-office & say, "Post this, you fool. *All* of it. *All* the way."

Remember us to your mother & father and Dennis. Tell him all the boys here fight with hatchets.

Love,
DYLAN.

I had been staying with Dylan in Laugharne before the next letter. We had read Rilke's Duino Elegies to each other in the look-out of Laugharne Castle perched on the wall over the estuary. The poems excited Dylan deeply, though he called Rilke ' a very odd boy indeed'.

The first verse of ' The Marriage of a Virgin' came with this letter, and the completed poem with the next.

The ' forced novel' is, of course, Adventures in the Skin Trade.

Laugharne, Sunday, 21 June 1941

My dear Vernon:

It was very nice seeing you those days. I loved Rilke and the scrabbling in the shrubbery and your Sea Music. I wish you could have stayed longer. Sorry for being so huffish and insultable that last night: you know how it is.

Ackerley has been in Laugharne for the last 3 days; or four. Funny, after our talking about him. Someone who stayed here last year told him about the place; he'd never heard of it before. He was sorry to miss you, here and in London: I told him you'd been in London & that you missed him here by one day only. He's quite a charming man, rather grey and tired, with a nice smile and a lazy, affected, very pleasant voice. About 50.

He said he liked your poems a great deal. Most of the time he was here he spent doing great walks, but I met him every evening in the pub and he came to the house for drinks.

Here is a tiny poem I've just done. Not very well formed; just a poem between bits of my unfortunately forced novel, a breathing space between mechanizations; & I think I agree with you about that destination phrase.

Do write soon; and tell me about going to London. We're just the same.

Love,
DYLAN.

Poem on back.

[*On back of letter:*]

THE MARRIAGE OF A VIRGIN.

Waking alone in a multitude of loves when morning's light
Surprised in the opening of her nightlong eyes
His shining yesterday asleep upon the iris
And this day's sun rode up the sky out of her thighs
Was miraculous virginity old as loaves and fishes,
Though the moment of a miracle is unending lightning
And the shipyards of Galilee's footprints hide a navy of doves.

Laugharne, Friday [July 3? 41]

Dear Vernon:

A wonderful surprise present. Thank you. I could buy Laugharne, but it would be ostentatious.

A great pity you couldn't come this weekend. Beforehand I miss you. And you'd have had the pleasure of Hughes's company. He's been aloofly here for some days. I don't know what he does on the Admiralty, but I can imagine him being introduced: "Ah, Admiral, and here's Hughes, Richard Hughes, you know, our Out of Contact man."

I'll try to come down next weekend, and thank you. If I

don't it will be because I'm in London; or, of course, because Marjorie's with you. I must go to London quickly, to see what honey of a ministerial job is open for a man of the strictest obscurity and intemperance: £1000 a year, excluding tips, bribes, blackmail, bloodmoney, petty cash, and profits realized by the sale of female clerks into the white slave traffic and the removal of office furniture.

I look forward to the new poem.

I'll write as soon as I know about my London visit.

Anyway, next weekend or the weekend of the 20th.

Thank you again,
Love,
DYLAN

I'm enclosing the short, now finished, poem.

[*Enclosed with letter:*]

THE MARRIAGE OF A VIRGIN

Waking alone in a multitude of loves when morning's light
Surprised in the opening of her nightlong eyes
His golden yesterday asleep upon the iris
And this day's sun leapt up the sky out of her thighs
Was miraculous virginity old as loaves and fishes
Though the moment of a miracle is unending lightning
And the shipyards of Galilee's footprints hide a navy of doves.

No longer will the vibrations of the sun desire on
Her deepsea pillow where once she married alone,
Her heart all ears and eyes, lips catching the avalanche
Of the golden ghost who ringed with his streams her mercury
    bone,
Who under the lids of her windows hoisted his golden luggage,
For a man sleeps where fire leapt down and she learns through
    his arm
That other sun, the jealous coursing of the unrivalled blood.

*Two well-known poems came with the next letter. The Park of
the second poem is Cwmdonkin Park, also mentioned in 'Once It
Was The Colour Of Saying', where Dylan played as a child. In
February 1943 Dylan read this poem on the wireless in the script
called 'Memories of Childhood'.*

Laugharne, Tuesday [1941, probably]

Dear V.

Here are two poems of very different kinds. That is to say,
here are two poems. Do tell me at *once* what you think of them.
I am a bit dubious about "Through ruin" in the third line of
the sextet. Originally I had "All day."

Looking forward to the weekend. As I told you, the only 2
things that will prevent me coming are London & utter poverty
(in which I am now, having to borrow 2 1/2d for this stamp)
But I do want to come. I'll ring up either on Thursday evening
or Friday morning. What's the trainfare?

Much love,
DYLAN

[Enclosed with this letter in typescript:]

AMONG THOSE KILLED IN THE DAWN
RAID WAS A MAN AGED A HUNDRED

When the morning was waking over the war
He put on his clothes and stepped out and he died,
The locks yawned loose and a blast blew them wide,
He dropped where he loved on the burst pavement stone
And the funeral grains of the slaughtered floor.
Tell his street on its back he stopped a sun
And the craters of his eyes grew springshoots and fire
When all the keys shot from the locks, and rang.

Dig no more for the chains of his grey haired heart.
The heavenly ambulance drawn by a wound
Through ruin waits for the spades' ring on the cage.

O keep his bones away from that common cart,
The morning is flying on the wings of his age
And a hundred storks perch on the sun's right hand.

THE HUNCHBACK IN THE PARK

The hunchback in the park
A solitary mister
Propped between trees and water
From the opening of the garden lock
That lets the trees and water enter
Until the Sunday sombre bell at dark,

Eating bread from a newspaper
Drinking water from the chained cup
That the children filled with gravel
In the fountain basin where I sailed my ship
Slept at night in a dog kennel
But nobody chained him up.

Like the park birds he came early
Like the water he sat down
And Mister they called hey mister
The truant boys from the town
Running when he had heard them clearly
On out of sound

Past lake and rockery
Laughing when he shook his paper
Hunchbacked in mockery
Through the loud zoo of the willow groves
Dodging the park keeper
With his stick that picked up leaves.

And the old dog sleeper
Alone between nurses and swans

While the boys among willows
Made the tiger jump out of their eyes
To roar on the rockery stones
And the groves were blue with sailors

Made all day until bell time
A woman figure without fault
Straight as a young elm
Straight and tall from his crooked bones
That she might stand in the night
After the lock and chains

All night in the unmade park
After the railings and shrubberies
The birds the grass the trees the lake
Had followed the hunchback
And the wild boys innocent as strawberries
To his kennel in the dark.

The poems of mine referred to in the next letter are 'Foal' and 'Money for the Market', both printed in The Lady With The Unicorn *in 1948.*

Laugharne, Wednesday [1941, probably]
Dear Vernon:
    Thank you for the lovely weekend. A pity we couldn't have done more, but I liked very much what we did. I *must* have a copy soon of the Foal which I remember, lots of it, by heart on a first hearing: nothing, perhaps, to old Datas Watkins but a great deal for me. I hope the Money poem goes well, and probably 'Earth-winged mortal' is right. It's just that to me it doesn't express the meaning you originally told me.
    Thank you for the croquet & the poems & the kindness & the money; and thank your mother for me, very much, for the

superabundance of far-too-good-for-the-war food. Remember me to your mother & Mr. Watkins & Dennis.

Yo— etc Lederer came down with me for 2 days & is returning tomorrow. He *walks*. A nice boy, but terribly affected in many ways. Dante is boring. Eliot is dry. Gorki is a journalist. But I think that what he really thinks, & will one day be brave enough to say, is simple, unaffected, & right.

Thank you for 'Assembling'. Of course.

A proper letter soon when I know more plans. And I hope I can send you a poem soon.

I liked everything.

Love,

DYLAN

& CAITLIN

& LLEW

c/o Horizon, 6 Selwyn House, Lansdowne Terrace, WC1

28 Aug 1941

My dear Vernon,

A tiny note to tell you where, if you write, I can be got hold of. It's only a forwarding address, I haven't moved into the editor's chair. The place I'm staying in in London is closed after tomorrow or Friday and we haven't yet found anywhere new. We've been having an awful time, and I have felt like killing myself. We arrived with no money, after leaving Llewelyn in Ringwood, and have had none since. In Laugharne that was not so bad. In stinking, friendless London it is unendurable. I am still looking for a film job, & have been offered several scripts to do "in the near future", which might mean weeks. In the meantime, we sit in our bedroom and think with hate of the people who can go to restaurants. Have you written? Frances Hughes has, as yet, forwarded no letters. I would have written to you long before, but have been too miserable even to write Poem at the top of a clean page and then look out of the window at the millionaires catching buses. Are you, I don't hope, in the army? Write soon. Soon perhaps this will have been worn away, hunger, anger, boredom, hate and unhappiness, and I will be able to write to you about all the things we have always had, and will always have, to talk about together. We are prisoners now in a live melodrama and all the long villains with three halfpence are grinning in at us through the bars. Not the best bars either. Bless you,

DYLAN.

After a long deferred service, I had left for the Air Force in December 1941. Although we continued to keep in touch, and to see each other fairly frequently, I lost all the letters that came during the next two and a half years.

Dan, mentioned in paragraph 7 of the next letter, is Dylan's lifelong friend, Dr. Daniel Jones, the composer, whose Fourth Symphony is dedicated to his memory. His parents lived in a house in Swansea called 'Warmley', the house described in the Portrait Of The Artist *story, 'The Fight'.*

The poem referred to in paragraph 8 is 'Ceremony After A Fire Raid', a printed cutting of which accompanied this letter.

———— *27 July 1944*

Dear Vernon,

I didn't think it was so long since we saw each other, or since I wrote to you. We were three months in Sussex, and two months near Beaconsfield. So it's nearly half a year and what a year and what a pity and what the hell. We must (always my fault that we haven't) write regularly to each other now, if only to report that a little tepid blood is still trickling, that there is still a faint stir somewhere in the chest, that we can still put pen to paper, paper to bottom, thumb to nose, the world to rights, two and two together, put and take.

The Sussex months were beastly. When it wasn't soaking wet, I was. Aeroplanes grazed the roofs, bombs came by night, police by day, there were furies at the bottom of my garden, with bayonets, and a floating dock like a kidney outside the window, and Canadians in the bushes, and Americans in the hair; it was a damned banned area altogether. They worshipped dogs there, too, and when a pom was born in one house the woman put out the Union Jack.

Near Beaconsfield, where Chesterton sat on his R.C., it was better. We stayed with a man who runs the film company I fool for, and the country was green and okay, but the well-off people were dry and thin and grieved over their petrolless motorcars and played bridge like ferrets, and the poor snarled and were all named Body.

Now we're with my mother and father in —— where everyone goes into the pubs sideways, & the dogs piss only on backdoors, and there are more unwanted babies shoved up the chimneys than there are used french letters in the offertory boxes. It's a mean place but near Laugharne where we will go next week.

Is Dot in Carmarthen? Let me know. We'd love to see her.

I've found that I can do most of my filmwork outside London, (which soon will be shelled terribly by things that scream up into the stratosphere, passing the queen bees, and then roar down on to Manresa Road), and so we are looking, again, for somewhere to live in the country. In Laugharne, if possible. In Wales, preferably. And we'll stay here, getting on my father —for he's one bald nerve—until we find a house, a flat, a room, a stye, a release.

By the way, I have a new complaint. Itching feet. There is nothing to see, the feet just itch. I have to take my shoes off many times a day and rub the soles with my socks. Ask Dan if he knows what it is—he's learned in little woes. How is Dan? I'd write to him but have lost his address. Ask him to write to me; I feel very Warmley to him all the time, and would very much love to hear.

Here is a poem (printed in 'Our Time') which perhaps you haven't seen. I didn't print the Lorca lines above the poem.

Will you tell me about it? It really is a Ceremony, and the third part of the poem is the music at the end. Would it be called a voluntary, or is that only music at the beginning?

I am writing poems, and have three new ones I'll send you when they are typewritten and after I have heard from you about the Ceremony.

Write very soon, please, & tell me everything.

Love,

DYLAN.

The poem of over 200 lines of the next letter is 'Vision And Prayer'.

Aeronwy, Dylan's daughter, was now a year old.

Blaen Cwm, Llangain, near Carmarthen, 26 August 1944

Dear Vernon,

I'm so very glad that you are going to Pennard on September 2nd, and that Gwen is coming down too and that we shall be able to see both of you. Do you think that you could come to Carmarthen town to meet? It's only an hour by bus from Swansea. We would come to Pennard but it's a nuisance taking the baby on crowded buses and my mother is never very well and it's rather a strain for her to look after Aeronwy for a whole day. If you come to Carmarthen we could meet in the Boar's Head or somewhere and have some beer in a corner and a long lunch. So please do try. I'll look forward to hearing from you. Bring a poem. I've just finished two poems, one over 200 lines and I'm excited by it. The other is a Laugharne poem: the first place poem I've written. I'll bring them both along.

We may be living in New Quay in a week or two, & are trying to get a house. If we do—the house will be right on the sea—you *must* come down to stay after you are married. Or before, of course, but I mean as a special bit of holiday.

Caitlin sends her love to both of you. And mine is sent always.

DYLAN.

No word from Dan. Do you see him. Or will you send his address.
I saw Mervyn Levy. He's stationed at Llangennech.
Keidrych is living in Llanybri again, but I don't see him much.
Our dog has got mange.
Aeronwy cannot walk but she climbs rocks.
And of course we are coming to your marriage, in our brightest colours.

The beautiful poem which accompanied the next letter had been contemplated for three years. Dylan later altered 'bare' trees to 'winged' and 'brown' in the fourth line from the end to 'leaved'.

Blaen Cwm, Llangain, Near Carmarthen.

Wednesday [30th August, 1944]

Dear Vernon,

A complication. On Monday Sept. 4 we are moving into a new house—we call it a house; it's made of wood and asbestos —in New Quay, Cardiganshire. It's in a really wonderful bit of the bay, with a beach of its own. Terrific. But it means that we're much further from Carmarthen. Now how can we meet? Can you come down here? You said you didn't want to spend your leave outside Pennard, but couldn't you spare us just *one* night in New Quay? We would love it so. Anyway, write. After Monday, our address will be Majoda, New Quay. The name is made of the beginnings of the names of the three children of the man who built the questionable house. I may alter the name to Catllewdylaer.

Here is a new poem. It's a month & a bit premature. I do hope you like it, & wd like very much to read it aloud to you.

115

Will you read it aloud too? It's got, I think, a lovely slow lyrical movement.

Write as soon as you can.

We must all meet.

Love,
DYLAN.

In the poem, I notice, on copying out, that I have made October trees bare. I'll alter later.

[Enclosed with this letter:]

It was my thirtieth year to heaven
Woke to my hearing from harbour and neighbour wood
And the mussel pooled and the heron
Priested shore
The morning beckon
With water praying and call of sea gull and rook
And the knock of sailing boats on the net webbed wall
Myself to set foot
That second
In the still sleeping town and set forth.

My birthday began with the water
Birds and the birds of the bare trees flying my name
Above the farms and the white horses
And I rose
In rainy autumn
And walked abroad in a shower of all my days.
High tide and the heron dived when I took the road
Over the border
And the gates
Of the town closed as the town awoke.

A springful of larks in a rolling
Cloud and the roadside bushes brimming with whistling

Blackbirds and the sun of October
Summery
On the hill's shoulder,
Here were fond climates and sweet singers suddenly
Come in the morning where I wandered and listened
To the rain wringing
Wind blow cold
In the wood faraway under me.

Pale rain over the dwindling harbour
And over the sea wet church the size of a snail
With its horns through mist and the castle
Brown as owls
But all the gardens
Of spring and summer were blooming in the tall tales
Beyond the border and under the lark full cloud.
There could I marvel
My birthday
Away but the weather turned around.

It turned away from the blithe country
And down the other air and the blue altered sky
Streamed again a wonder of summer
With apples
Pears and red currants
And I saw in the turning so clearly a child's
Forgotten mornings when he walked with his mother
Through the parables
Of sun light
And the legends of the green chapels

And the twice told fields of infancy
That his tears burned my cheeks and his heart moved in mine.
These were the woods the river and sea
Where a boy
In the listening

Summertime of the dead whispered the truth of his joy
To the trees and the stones and the fish in the tide.
        And the mystery
          Sang alive
Still in the water and singingbirds.

      And there could I marvel my birthday
Away but the weather turned around. And the true
        Joy of the long dead child sang burning
          In the sun.
        It was my thirtieth
Year to heaven stood there in the summer noon
Though the town below was brown with October blood.
        O may my heart's truth
          Still be sung
On this high hill in a year's turning.

GRYPHON FILMS, *2-6 West Street, London, W.C.2*

TO BE READ FIRST

as from Majoda, New Quay, Cardiganshire, 28 Oct. 1944
My dear Gwen and Vernon,

What on earth can you think of me? It is the last, last, last thing of all—on top of all the other things—that the hasty letter I should scribble in such a panic to you, while on the train away from London where we never met, should remain unposted until today: 26 days after your wedding. I have no excuses, but that I was so flurried and anxious, so tired, so miserable, that I put the train-letter into my pocket, arrived in New Quay after an 8 hour journey, imagined, in a kind of delirium, that it was posted, & then waited, perhaps without much hope of ever hearing, to hear from you that, though I was not forgiven, my explanation was understood. What can you think of me? Today I found the letter, crumpled, unposted, in my overcoat. Please, please do try to understand.

I shall let you have these two letters now, & a poem I meant also to send weeks ago, without another word of apology or abasement. All our love to you both, for your happiness forever.

Your worst man,
DYLAN

[*Sent with letter dated 28 October 1944:*]
[*pencil*]   *The Train to Wales, 1.30 Wed.*

ON NOT TURNING UP TO BE BEST MAN AT THE WEDDING OF ONE'S BEST FRIEND

Reeking & rocking back from a whirled London where nothing went right, all duties were left, and my name spun rank in the whole old smoky nose, I try, to a rhythm of Manchester pocket-hankerchers, and Conk him on the mousetrap, Conk him on the mousetrap, from the London-leaving wheels, to explain to you both, clearly & sincerely, why I never arrived, in black overcoat & shiny suit, rose-lapelled, breathing cachous & great good will, at lunch and church. But the train's stacked tight, I'm tabling a bony knee for this little pad, and am stuck, in the windy corridor, between many soldiers, all twelve foot high & commando-trained to the last lunge of the bayonet. It's not easy to think, or write, or be, and my explanations, true as air, sound, when I try to marshall them, like a chapter of accidents written in a dream by a professor of mathematics who has forgotten all formulas but the wrong one that 2 & 2 make 5. First, then, I arrived in London on Thursday & was sent straightaway, that is, on Friday morning, to Coventry: the City of Coventry, where the company who pay me occasionally are making a film called 'Building The Future', a subject on which I particularly should have no say. In Coventry I arranged to catch a train back on Sunday night, which would carry me to London in time to meet you both at the station. That train, owing to no fault of my own but to callous &

diffident members of the hotel staff, who did not trouble to get the train-times straight, but only late, I missed. There was no other train until the next morning, which was Monday, & that train would reach London at an hour just convenient for me to be able to get into a cab & race for the church. I could not, at that hour of Sunday night, reach my office to leave a message for someone there to spend Monday morning ringing up you & your people & making my—by this time—frantic excuses; I could, indeed, have reached the office by telephone, but there would be no-one there to answer, except some celluloid rat or other. So I waited until Monday morning & then, before catching the train, rang up the office & told a secretary girl to ring Charing Cross Hotel straight away, get in touch with anyone called Watkins, & explain the whole position to him or her.

I had not, myself, got the time to ring up Charing X Hotel, as it wd take hours, & as my call to the office could be, & was, made Priority, thereby saving those hours during which, by the nicotine-stained skin of my few teeth, I caught the wedding-going & troop-crammed horribly slow train. On arriving in London I managed, by the fervour of my heart only, I am sure, to snatch a cab. I sat back, wheezing, in it. "Where to?" the driver said. And—this is the real God-help-me—I couldn't remember the name of the church. It was after half past one. I looked in all my pockets but had left your last letter, I suppose, in wood-&-asbestos Majoda, New Quay. I tried, in my head, every church name I knew. I explained to the driver: "A Church in the City. Very old." Suddenly something came & I said, "I think it's Godolphin. Or something like that. Yes, Godolphin." We went to the City, the driver was dubious. We asked policemen: they were certain. By now, after two, & you too, I feared & hoped, married without my presence but with all my love, I went back to the office to find the secretary-girl out for lunch & the few people still there surprisingly cool and ignorant of all the infernal muddle that had been clotting up the wheels of the world for over a day. There was nothing

to do. When the girl came in I asked her, though I was terrified
to ask, if her little side of the whole business had gone well.
She had tried the Charing X Hotel all the morning. The
Watkins were out. She had left my name. The Watkins were
out.

Later that evening, feeling wretcheder than ever before,
alone in my beast of a studio, I remembered the church. Of
course I remembered the church. Not Godolphin but St.
Bartholomew the Great—too late! O what a prize of prize
pickles & I'll understand always if you never want to see me
again. I know this hasty jumble can't explain all the somersault-
ing & backspinning of circumstance against my being where I
most wanted to be: at your wedding. God bless you both, & do
try to forgive me.

All my love,

DYLAN.

*With the last letter came the typescript of the poem 'Vision and
Prayer'. It is identical with the published version, with an ex-
planatory note on the back to show how the poem should be set
out.*

*The 'David' poem of mine to which the next letter refers is
'Reprisals Of Calm', printed in* The Lady With The Unicorn.

Majoda, New Quay, Cardiganshire, Nov. 15 1944

[*pencil*]
Dear Vernon,

I was so very pleased to have your letter last week, your
letter this morning, and, best, yours and Gwen's (even in
1980) pardon. I can now take my head out of the grubby lining
of my overcoat pocket, where I have been keeping it for weeks
along with a beetle, something that looks like porridge and
smells like the underground, and an unposted letter. I can
take my head out now and face the perpetual rain.

I like your address, especially if it is Story Stratford. What kind of a house have you, or is it a room, or rooms, or a flat, or the use of somebody's old larder to live in? I should like very much to visit you, if I may, one day, soon, in December. Caitlin and I are going to London the first week of December. Caitlin will leave Aeronwy with her mother, at Ringwood, and we will probably stay in an hotel for a week or two. Caitlin hasn't had a holiday away from Aeronwy since Aeronwy appeared with pain and trumpets. So we want to go to cinemas & theatres and eat nice spicy meals and meet you and Gwen and go to see paintings and drink in the Eight Bells and Claridges like improper people and sneer at the V.2. and come back here for Christmas. (I didn't tell you that Vera Phillips, now Killick, for she has married a man called Killick but who, for years, we thought was called Waistcoat, is living in the next bungalow to us on this ratty cliff. She lives alone except for her baby daughter who is five months old and, during all that time, has screamed only twice. Vera says it is because of character. We say it is because of laziness. Vera lives on cocoa, and reads books about the technique of third century brass work, and gets up only once a day to boil the cat an egg, which it detests.) So we must meet in London. Is it possible for you & Gwen to have leave together & come up and see a play in a theatre, or outside a theatre, with us? And a real meal, not a crawl on bent minds round the Tambied pubs?

Has Dot told you yet that we met in Cardigan, filthy town, for a, on my part, rather rambling hour? I had been to a farmer's fair. Dot looked awfully well, and was lovely to meet. I hope I'll see her again when she comes billeting.

I am so glad you liked the 'Vision & Prayer' poem; and that the diamond shape of the first part seems no longer to you to be cramped & artificed. I agree that the second part is, formally, less inevitable, but I cannot alter it, except, perhaps, in detail. I will read the very last line again, & see what, if anything, can be done about the stresses. I haven't a copy of the poem with me but, as I remember, I liked the last line *for*

the awkward stressing, for the braking, for the slowing up of
the last two same-vowelled ~~birds~~ words (I wrote 'birds' instead of 'words'). But I'll read the whole poem again, most
carefully. Yes, the Hound of Heaven is baying there in the last
verse, but, at the moment, and again from memory, I don't
remember seeing any Hopkins after the poem was finished.

I'll look out for the David poem in the Listener, if I can get
a copy from our newsagent who closes nearly all day and sells,
I think, only the Western Mail and ink.

Here is a poem of mine which I started a long time ago but
finished very recently, after a lot of work. This poem, the
Vision & Prayer, & the birthday poem are coming out together
in the January Horizon. I hope you'll be able to get a copy &
see them in pretty print.

How is Dan? Is he a new father? Do you see him? Send him
my love, if you do.

And love from Caitlin & myself to you and Gwen.

Ever,
DYLAN.

[Enclosed with this letter or the next, dated 28 Nov. 1944]

HOLY SPRING

O
Out of a bed of love
When that immortal hospital made one more move to soothe
The cureless counted body,
And ruin and his causes
Over the barbed and shooting sea assumed an army
And swept into our wounds and houses,
I climb to greet the war in which I have no heart but only
That one dark I owe my light,
Call for confessor and wiser mirror but there are none
To glow after the god stoning night
And I am struck as lonely as a holy maker by the sun.

No

Praise that the spring time is all
Gabriel and radiant shrubbery as the morning grows joyful
Out of the woebegone pyre
And the multitude's sultry tear turns cool on the weeping wall,
My arising prodigal
Sun the father his quiver full of the infants of pure fire,
But blessed be hail and upheaval
That uncalm still it is sure alone to stand and sing
Alone in the husk of man's home
And the mother and toppling house of the holy spring,
If only for a last time.

Majoda, New Quay, Cardiganshire, Tue. Nov. 28. 44
Dear Vernon,

I hope you find the poem visible this time.

I will be in London from December the first: for, say, ten days. (Though I don't know why, 'say'). Will you wire me, any day after the first, at

GRYPHON 2-6 WEST STREET W.C.2.

and say when you & Gwen can come up. I suggest either Monday, Dec. 4, Tuesday, Dec. 5, or Wednesday, Dec. 6. I suggest one o'clock (1 p.m.) as the time, and the Back Bar of the Cafe Royal (table facing the door) as the place. If you can meet *there*, at *that* time, on *any* of the three days suggested above, your wire need contain only the one word—Monday (or Tuesday, of course, or Wednesday)—and I shall be there— (Back Bar of the Cafe Royal, table facing door, one p.m.)— henna'd, camelia'd, & smelling of moths.

I shall buy the December Horizon for your poem. How big is it? Send, by rail, or carrier pigeon, or in a plain man, a prose summary of all your poems and a pocket bicycle and a machine for draining witches and oh God help me I should never write letters after lunch: I am whimsical, I am porky, there are peas in my ears & my smile is gravy.

Yes, we could see 'Night at the Opera', I should love that, or a murder film called 'Laura', or even Henry V.

I am *very* frightened of the rockets.

There is no news here: a woman called Mrs. Prosser died in agony last week, there has been a coroner's inquest on a drowned coastguard (verdict suicide), Vera's cat was wounded by a rabbit trap & died, all night long we hear rabbits shrieking like babies in the steel jaws in the hedges, Caitlin killed five mice in one day by traps, but, still, I am quite happy and am looking forward to a gross, obscene and extremely painful middle-age.

Did I tell you I was going to Ireland early next year: to an island off Kerry? Well, I am, & I shall tell you about it when we meet.

Wire me after the first, at the unlikely address of GRYPHON, 2-6 West St., W.C.2.

Love to you both from Caitlin & myself.

Ever,
DYLAN.

The next letter was written after an incident of a violent nature which caused Dylan distress and made his sense of danger more immediate. Such incidents were not uncommon in war-time and in his experience, but this one was more than usually acute.

The long poem sent with the next letter is one of his master-pieces, 'A Winter's Tale'. There are only two lines which differ from the final form of the poem:

Line 2 of verse 14: 'a' *was afterwards changed to* 'the' *in this line:* 'In a long ago land' *became:* 'In the long ago land'; *and line 2 of verse 7, where the word* 'made' *was afterwards changed to* 'veiled' *sky:*

He wept from the crest of grief, he prayed to the made sky

With 'A Winter's Tale' came the three short poems, 'The Conversation Of Prayers'—the title was later changed to 'The

Conversation of Prayer', 'This Side Of The Truth', and 'A Refusal To Mourn The Death, By Fire, Of A Child In London'. There are small differences between this version of 'The Conversation Of Prayers' and the final text of the poem, but the other two poems remained unchanged except that a comma was put at the end of the first line of the poem for Llewelyn.

Majoda, New Quay, Cardiganshire, 28 March 1945

My dear Vernon,

Lovely to hear from you. I'd have written before this but ... ... and Caitlin and I go to bed under the bed. The last letter I wrote to you, at Pennard, told of my daily terrors, my everyday traps and pits, [etc.] I'm sure you thought I was exxagerating [sic]. At debts' and death's door I now stand with a revolving stomach, waiting for V.1000 and the Bubonic Plague.

How are you both? I miss seeing you, but then I have missed seeing you properly for—what is it—years; at least, since we left our studio, where we did have some proper evenings. The war's over soon, let's see each other then, a lot. You'll be going back to Swansea, of course. I want to stay in Wales for a bit, too. The Irish trip is off until the summer, & perhaps until even later.

Give my love, when you write, to your Mother and Father. My Father is awfully ill these days, with heart disease and uncharted pains, and the world that was once the colour of tar is now a darker place.

I'm sending you some new poems. The long one doesn't, I think, come off, but I like it all in spite of that. It isn't really one piece, though, God, I tried to make it one and have been working on it for months. Do tell me all you think of it, and of the others. And do let me see some of your new poems, please. Write very soon.

Love from both to both,

Ever,
DYLAN.

James Laughlin, of New Directions, America, who is going
to bring out a book of mine, "Selected Writings", in America,
wants, from a friend of mine over here, a short, "personal
introduction" to the book, *of not more than 1000 words*. There
is a "critical introduction", but that Laughlin is having written by an American, J. L. Sweeney. Laughlin has just written
to me to say that he must have this "personal" thing at once.
Could you do it, or, rather, would you like to do it, or, rather,
have you got time to do it, or, again, could you make or find
time to do it. What Laughlin means by a "personal introduction" is, roughly, this—I quote from memory as I haven't got
the letter here—:

"an idea, in non highbrow language, of what you yourself are
really like; a human portrait of the poet written by a close
friend of his or by one who has known him for a long time."
You'll have to excuse phrases like "non highbrow language",
"human portrait", etc, but what he really wants is clear, I
think. American readers of poetry seem never to be really
satisfied unless they have portraits—photograph or words—
of the writers; and they like them as candid and intimate—
comic, if you see me that way, & you must do, sometimes—as
possible. To me, of course, that introduction coming from you,
as my friend and as—we've both said this, with a kind of
giggling gravity—the only other poet except me whose poetry
I really like today—would be the best in the world. Let me
know if you would do it; and, if you would, could you do it
terribly quickly and let me have it so that I can send it off
almost at once. It's a lot to ask, and you hardly ever write prose,
but. . . . Well, I'll hear from you. We know each other by
doing so many things together, from croquet to bathing (me
for the first time) in the icy moon, poetry and very high teas,
getting drunk, reading, reading, reading, sea staring, Swansea,
Gower, Laugharne, London . . . I've written thousands of
letters to you; if you've kept some you could use what you

liked to help build up this "human portrait" of this fat
pleader,

Write very soon.

[*Sent with letter of 28 March 1945:*]

THE CONVERSATION OF PRAYERS

The conversation of prayers about to be said
By the child going to bed and the man on the stairs
Who climbs to his dying love in her high room,
The one not caring to whom in his sleep he will move
And the other full of tears that she will be dead,

Turns in the dark on the sound they know will arise
Into the answering skies from the green ground,
From the man on the stairs and the child by his bed.
The sound about to be said in the two prayers
For the sleep in a safe land and the love who dies

Will be the same grief flying. Who shall they calm?
Shall the child sleep unharmed or the man be crying?
The conversation of prayers about to be said
Turn on the quick and the dead, and the man on the stairs
To-night shall find no dying but alive and warm

In the fire of his care his love in the high room.
And the child not caring to whom he climbs his prayer
Shall drown in a grief as deep as his made grave.
And mark the dark eyed wave, through the eyes of sleep
Dragging him up the stairs to one who lies dead.

A REFUSAL TO MOURN THE DEATH, BY FIRE, OF A CHILD IN LONDON

Never until the mankind making
Bird beast and flower
Fathering and all humbling darkness
Tells with silence the last light breaking
And the still hour
Is come of the sea tumbling in harness

And I must enter again the round
Zion of the water bead
And the synagogue of the ear of corn
Shall I let pray the shadow of a sound
Or sow my salt seed
In the least valley of sackcloth to mourn

The majesty and burning of the child's death.
I shall not murder
The mankind of her going with a grave truth
Nor blaspheme down the stations of the breath
With any further
Elegy of innocence and youth.

Deep with the first dead lies London's daughter,
Robed in the long friends,
The grains beyond age, the dark veins of her mother,
Secret by the unmourning water
Of the riding Thames.
After the first death, there is no other.

THIS SIDE OF THE TRUTH

(for Llewelyn)
This side of the truth
You may not see, my son,
King of your blue eyes

In the blinding country of youth,
That all is undone,
Under the unminding skies,
Of innocence and guilt
Before you move to make
One gesture of the heart or head,
Is gathered and spilt
Into the winding dark
Like the dust of the dead.

Good and bad, two ways
Of moving about your death
By the grinding sea,
King of your heart in the blind days,
Blow away like breath,
Go crying through you and me
And the souls of all men
Into the innocent
Dark, and the guilty dark, and good
Death, and bad death, and then
In the last element
Fly like the stars' blood,

Like the sun's tears,
Like the moon's seed, rubbish
And fire, the flying rant
Of the sky, king of your six years.
And the wicked wish
Down the beginning of plants
And animals and birds,
Water and light, the earth and sky,
Is cast before you move,
And all your deeds and words,
Each truth, each lie,
Die in unjudging love.

The American edition of Dylan Thomas's Selected Writings, *published by New Directions in November 1946, with an introduction by J. L. Sweeney, did not afterwards use a personal note. I did write one, to which the next letter alludes, but I did not, so far as I can remember, quote from any of his letters. Nor was the note at all adequate or satisfactory, for what one is asked to do is never either, unless it is done without embarrassment. My own embarrassment was acute, like that of a man holding a many-coloured kite on a windless day.*

Majoda, April 19   45

Dear Vernon,

It was so good of you to write that little personal—what?—thing, then, so quickly and so very nicely. Just, I should imagine, what New Directions want, and I have sent it off *just* as it is, not even altering 'good' to 'great' or putting in a paragraph about my singing voice or horsemanship. Thank you a lot. It did, I know, sound rather awful: Write about me. If you had asked me to do it about you, I think I should have pleaded everything from writer's cramp to never having met you except in the dark, & then only once. I'm so glad you wrote the last bit about the poems: how you so much more liked the latest to the earliest. Wouldn't it be hell if it was the other way around, and the words were coming quicker & slicker and weaker and wordier every day and, by comparison, one's first poems in adolescence seemed, to one, like flying-fish islands never to be born in again? Thank God, writing is daily more difficult, less passes Uncle Head's blue-haired pencil that George Q. Heart doesn't care about, and that the result, if only to you and me, is worth all the discarded shocks, the reluctantly shelved grand moony images, cut-&-come again cardpack of references.

And I'm very glad you liked the new poems I sent, especially A Winter's Tale. I won't be able to test your suggestions for myself until I have the proofs back from Dent: I seem to have lost other copies. My book should be out this spring,

I*   131

costing, luckily, three and six so that perhaps lots of people can buy it and pass it on.

Yes,——has nearly put me off drinking, though, indeed, the night of the shots of the dark I had drunk only some bottled cider and talked morosely to retired sailors in dusty corners, provoking nobody, so I thought.

I do hope I see you soon in Stony Stratford. I am going to London the end, perhaps, of next week.

Thank you again for the little personal what; it was, I thought, nice, funny, and, as far as I know, right.

I'll write again, very soon, and more.

Love,

DYLAN.

Majoda, New Quay, Cardiganshire, May 21. 1945

Dear Vernon:

Lovely to hear from you. I wish I could come to Pennard to see you, but I am broke & depressed & have just returned from London & hated it more than ever & though it is lovely here I am not. Oh, I do wish *you* could come down here. There is room, rest, food, & sea. Can't you?

Just a tiny note. I'm worried about things. I think I'll walk & grieve and scowl at the unmitigated birds—the first adjective, of any kind, I cd think of.

Can't you come down? *Try.*

My love, & Caitlin's, to your people and yourself.

DYLAN

My paper on Wilfred Owen, written ten years earlier, which Dylan had read at Pennard, and which I later read at Oxford, had been stored in a friend's house with other things during the war, and a long search failed to produce it. It turned up again, when I was not looking for it, two or three years later.

Alfred Janes had been, before the war, a fantastically slow painter, working seven or eight hours a day for perhaps six months at a single picture, usually at that time a still life, a geometrical study of fish or fruit. His close friend Tom Warner, whose musical composition had given Dylan the title of his story 'A Prospect Of The Sea', had left Swansea and was teaching in England.

Holywell Ford, Oxford, April 27th 1946

My dear Vernon,

There's never been such a long time between our letters, and I hope, atom willing, there won't be again. (Somewhere in the wet Magdalen trees a bird makes a noise exactly like Doctor Ludwig Koch). It's been my fault of course, that goes without whining, but I'm heavy with reasons like Doctor Magnus Hirschfeld.

Right below where we live—it is, I think, a converted telephone kiosk, with a bed where the ledge for directories used to be—there is a vole-run. (Do not tell this to Fred who said that I could not speak for half a minute without mentioning vermin or Dracula, and that was five years ago). The run is so narrow that two voles cannot pass each other. Suddenly, an elderly, broad vole with a limp came quite fast down the run from the left just as an elderly, broader vole with a limp came from the right. From where I am sitting, expectantly nervous and ill like patients on an imminent, I could see what the voles were thinking. They never stopped running as they thought, as they neared one another. Who was to turn back? should they both turn back? should they fight, kiss, call it a day, lie down? They never stopped their limping running as I saw and heard the decision made. With a wheezing like that of a little otter, with a husky squeaky updrawing of shining arthritic legs, the elderly broader limping vole jumped over the back of the other. Not a word was said.

We've been here about six weeks, just behind Magdalen, by river and vole-run, very quiet, Aeronwy in a day-nursery near and sleeping in the next-door house or house-proper, Caitlin and I going our single way into the vegetable kingdom. I haven't worked for a long time, apart from reading, every week, over the air to the Indians: an audience of perhaps three, and all of them bat-or-Tambi-voiced. I'm reading Hardy on the ordinary service on May 19th. Probably about eleven at night. Try to remember to listen. I've written a long comic poem, not to be published, to keep the uttermost cellarmen of depression away and to prevent my doing crosswords. I've written a few pieces, nearly all quotations, for the Eastern radio, on Edward Thomas, Hardy, and some others. And I'm going to do a programme on Wilfred Owen: though all my job is the selection of the poems for professional readers to (badly, usually) read, and the interpolation of four-line comments between each. I'd love to see your essay on Owen. Could I? I'd be very careful with it and return it spotlessly unAeron-wied. And I want to write a poem of my own again, but it's hard here with peace and no room, spring outside the window and the gas cooker behind the back, sleep, food, loud wireless, broom and brush all in one kiosk, stunted bathing-hut or square milkbottle.

About Owen: Siegfried Sassoon has a lovely chapter about him, completely new, in his latest book, Siegfried's Journey. You would like it very much.

It's strange to think of you, and Fred, and Tom sometimes, in Swansea again. How is that blizzardly painter, that lightning artist, that prodigal canvas-stacker? Has he reached the next finbone of the fish he was dashing off before the war? Please give him my love.

And Cwmdonkin Park. I wish we were there now. Next month some-time I'm going down to see my mother, who has been very very ill, outside Carmarthen, and will stop at Swansea on the way back? Have you a little sheetless, must be sheetless, dogbox with nails for me to sleep in? Any shelter for a night? Unless you've been mending the roof. Then we could, maybe, all spend one evening together, wipey-eyed, remembering, locked in these damned days, the as-then-still-forgiven past.

You and Fred and Tom and, shame, no Dan whose future's stranger than ever, his symphonies shouldering out in his head to unplayable proportions, his officer's trousers kept up now by three safety-pins. And me too: I had a little time in hospital but I'm out again now and fit as an old potato.

Love to you all, Gwen, Rhiannon, yourself, from Caitlin, Llewelyn—in Cornwall for a month—, Aeronwy and myself. Please do send a photograph of Rhiannon. And the Owen?

DYLAN.

Blaen Cwm, Llangain, near Carmarthen, 26th August 1946.
My dear Vernon,

I'm a little nearer Swansea, anyway, and I hope to see you at the end of this week or the beginning of next. I'd have written from Ireland but I didn't take letters or anything with me and couldn't remember your address. V. Watkins, Swansea, looked presumptuous. Ireland was lovely. We spent all our time in Dublin and in Kerry. We ate ourselves daft: lobsters, steaks, cream, hills of butter, homemade bread, chicken and chocolates: we drank Seithenyns of porter and Guinness: we walked, climbed, rode on donkeys, bathed, sailed, rowed, danced, sang. I wish you'd been there. I didn't write anything, but here in Wales I will—all about Ireland. It'll be lovely to see you all, and so soon. I'll let you know exactly when.

Best love,
DYLAN.

'Bush' in line 2 of the next letter refers to the Bush Hotel in Swansea, where Dylan used to stay, and where we often met.

Dylan had come to Swansea to collect information for his script 'Return Journey', and particularly to check the pre-war order of the shops in the streets which had been completely demolished by bombs. This script is included in the collection Quite Early One Morning.

Dylan took the chief part in the broadcast of my Ballad of the Mari Lwyd *in the Third Programme soon after this letter was written. Unfortunately no record of his magnificent reading in this part has been preserved.*

Holywell Ford, Oxford, March 16. 1947

Dear Vernon,

It was lovely, all those weeks ago in the snow, to see you and talk and laugh, Bush, water-pistol, Fred (Fish) Janes, and all. I was sorry not to be able to come out to Pennard on my last evening: I lost the address, and had to go and see a master from the Swansea Grammar School to find out how much of the school was burned. "Bloody near all", he said; then, with a nasty sigh, he added, "All except Grey Morgan".

Thank you very much for wanting to buy Llewelyn a book for his Christmas Birthday. I'd like him to have a Bible too. But I'll ask him, in a minute—he's downstairs, playing Demon Rummy—and I hope he won't say Arthur Rackham [Ransome?] who he thinks [he] is the best writer in the universe except the writer of the Dick Barton series.

God brought a new one out of his bag of storms last night, tore down the trees and dropped one on our roof, flooded the only path, drove the voles to the trees, broke a window, sent Caitlin flying. I'd like to see Pennard now.

My Swansea programme was postponed because of fuel & weather, too little one, too much other, and can now be heard on April 2nd.

We go to Italy on April 8, but not to Florence: to a village near Rapallo. I shall ask about Pound.

I want very much to come & see you after April 2nd— The broadcast is from Cardiff—and will wire you at once if I can.

I'm looking forward to hearing 'Mari Lwyd' on Thursday. I'm one of the readers. I hope you won't mind too much.

136

Llewelyn's just sent his love, thanked you very much, and said:

I do hope I can see you soon.

Ever,
DYLAN.

The 'Old Age' programme referred to in the next letter was a broadcast in the Home Service, produced by Patric Dickinson, who had also produced my Mari Lwyd Ballad. *The readers of the poems were Dylan and V. C. Clinton-Baddeley, and I read the prose.*

On the day after the broadcast I went to Paris to read a paper on Yeats to the British Council. Before I left London Dylan told me that he would not be going to Paris after all. His reading, which was to have been held three weeks later, was cancelled.

The poem in Horizon *was 'In Country Sleep'.*

Manor House, South Leigh, Witney, Oxon. April 17. 48.
Dear Vern,

I'm going to write an enormous letter, very soon, to make up for this long long but never unthinking silence. I haven't written a letter longer than a page for oh dear! years, I think. And I'll send my new poem too. The long one in Horizon had 16 misprints, including Jew for dew. They are bringing out the poem as a broadcast, to placate me, though I'm not cross.

This is only to say, *Of course*, please use my Man Aged A Hundred in your Old Age programme, and I'm glad and proud you want it, and that I shall definitely be one of the readers in the programme. I'll love that.

Will you write & tell me when you will be in London, before or after Paris: preferably both. And I will come up, and we'll meet and talk and blare & whimper.

We're going to Paris at the end of May, for the British pretty Council. Wish it was when you were there. We are staying, for no reason, at the Hungarian Embassy. Or perhaps I am someone else.

Llewelyn (to go, next term, to Magdalen School), Aeronwy, Caitlin & me, who are all well, send our love to Gwen, Rhiannon, Gareth, and you. There's names!

See you soon, and I'll write *enormously* soon, too.

DYLAN.

Manor House, South Leigh, Witney, Oxon. Nov. 23, 48

Dear Vern,

Thank you for coming to the lunch. Thank you for writing and for remembering the book. Last week I bought it and left it, *at once*, in a cab. Before I had opened it. I left also Robert Graves's Collected Poems, Betjeman's Selected Poems, two library books about sudden death, somebody else's scarf and my own *my own* hat. Now I must wait till Christmas to read you. 'Cave Drawing', & 'Llewelyn's Chariot', I have, and one of the Carmarthen poems in an anthology. But I want all. I'll ask your godson about an annual when he comes back from school. It's games morning. He hates it, can't kick or throw. All he can do is dribble. Also he draws good engines, likes arithmetic, says Yah about poems, & Wizard about aeroplanes, Dick Barton, Up the Pole, tinned spaghetti, walnuts, and the caravan where I now, dear help me, work. Nothing happens to me. I go to London and bluster, come back and sigh, do a little scriptwriting, look at an unfinished poem, go out on my bicycle in the fog, go to London & bluster.

Mervyn Levy wrote to me yesterday. I wish Fred would write. I would to him if I had his address. And to Dan. My mother's no better, and will probably have to go to hospital again very soon. My father's better & naggier. I wish you had heard my story about Rhossili. I wish I were in Rhossili. I wish we saw each other oftener. Next Spring we will, in Laugharne and in Swansea. I'm so cold this morning I could sing an opera, all the parts, and do the orchestra with my asthma.

Write soon. Love to you all from us all.

Ever,
DYLAN.

The next letter refers to my book, The Lady with the Unicorn *which Faber's had published in October.*

'Rag-&-bone shop of the heart' is the end of Yeats' great poem, 'The Circus Animals' Desertion', to me his truest and most complete epitaph.

Manor House, South Leigh, Witney, Oxon 13 Dec. 1948

Dear Vernon,

Lovely book. Thank you very very much. I am reading it from the beginning, some every night, slow & light & lifted. I saw the review in the Times Literary Supplement & liked its praise but not all its detail; & pre-"Raphaelitism" is barmy. I'll write again when I've read all the (to me) new beautiful poems.

Llewelyn's Annual: he says there is something called "Science & Wonder" (Number 2. Very important, number 2.) Or anything, and he thanks you from his rag-&-bone shop.

All well but poor and tired here. I am sorry, I do not mean my mother is well, poor thing, she's as ill as a ward.

Love to all from us all,
Ever,
DYLAN.

The next and last letter is a note thanking me for writing to him on the death of his father.

The broadcast of my three ballads, 'Rough Sea', 'Three

Coins', and 'Hunt's Bay' in which Dylan read the poems and I the introductions, was not recorded.

Boat House, Laugharne, Carmarthenshire,
29 December 1952

Dear Vernon,

Thank you so much. I miss him a great deal.

This is only a little—after, years?—to say Happy New Year to you & Gwen & the children.

I hope I'll see you soon. I am going to read 3 ballads of yours from Swansea on the 14th of January. Can we meet for lunch that day?

It will be wonderful to see you again.

Ever,
DYLAN.

APPENDIX

INDEX

143